Sara Teasdale

Twayne's United States Authors Series

Kenneth Eble, Editor

University of Utah

TUSAS 509

SARA TEASDALE
(1884–1933)
Photograph courtesy of
AP/Wide World Photos

Sara Teasdale

By Carol B. Schoen

Herbert H. Lehman College
City University of New York

Twayne Publishers
A Division of G.K. Hall & Co. • Boston

Sara Teasdale

Carol B. Schoen

Copyright © 1986 by G.K. Hall & Co.
All Rights Reserved
Published by Twayne Publishers
A Division of G.K. Hall & Co.
70 Lincoln Street
Boston, Massachusetts 02111

Copyediting supervised by Lewis DeSimone
Book production by Elizabeth Todesco
Book design by Barbara Anderson

Typeset in 11 pt. Garamond
by Modern Graphics, Inc., Weymouth, Massachusetts

Printed on permanent/durable acid-free paper
and bound in the United States of America

Library of Congress Cataloging in Publication Data

Schoen, Carol.
  Sara Teasdale.

  (Twayne's United States authors series; TUSAS 509)
  Bibliography: p. 185
  Includes index.
  1. Teasdale, Sara, 1884–1933—Criticism and
interpretation.   I. Title.   II. Series.
PS3539.E15Z88   1986   811'.52   86–9835
ISBN 0–8057–7473–4

Contents

About the Author

Carol B. Schoen received her B.A. degree from Radcliffe College in 1948. In 1961, she resumed her education at Columbia University, receiving her Ph.D. in 1968 from the graduate faculties in English and Comparative Literature. Since 1968, she has taught at Herbert H. Lehman College, City University of New York, in the English and Academic Skills/SEEK Departments. She is the author of *Anzia Yezierska,* published in Twayne's United States Authors Series, and coauthor of *The Writing Experience* and *Thinking and Writing in College,* published by Little, Brown and Co.

Preface

At one time, Sara Teasdale was one of the most popular poets in the United States, admired by critics and the reading public alike. While scholars, for the most part, have ceased noticing her achievements, readers have continued to read her poems, necessitating more than twenty-five reprintings of her *Collected Poems* during the past fifty years. This study is written in the hope of restoring the critical acceptance her poetry deserves.

The revolution in poetry that occurred during Teasdale's lifetime helps explain the eclipse of her reputation. The work of Pound and Eliot and the Imagists elevated new standards by which to judge poetry and discounted the old values. The concern for metrical correctness, for purity of intent, and, above all, for melodic harmony gave way to a demand for concreteness, for rhythms composed "in the sequence of the musical phrase, not in the sequence of the metronome," for poetry that was "hard and clear."[1] Instead of proprieties of good taste and personal reticence, the new poets chose psychological probing and outspoken statement. The modified acceptance of these standards by poets like Teasdale, who had perfected their talents under the aegis of the old standards, went unnoticed while the more daring pronouncements were difficult, if not impossible, for them to follow. The precision of Teasdale's words, her use of natural diction and newer subject matter, the subtle harmonies of her lyrics, her extraordinary ability to follow form without being fettered by it, were no longer treated with respect.

Even when modernist standards were modified, the second-class status assigned to the poetry of women continued to limit the critical attention given to Teasdale's work. Although a few women, such as Marianne Moore, who eschewed the "feminine lyric" managed to be considered part of the mainstream of American poetry, most women poets continued to be treated with condescension. As late as 1959, a critic writing about Louise Bogan could condemn the "aesthetic and moral shortcomings" of women's poetry: "the spinning out; the embroidering of trivial themes; a concern with the mere surfaces of life."[2] Under the circumstances, Teasdale's technical skill and intelligence failed to attract attention.

Feminist critics have made great strides in recent years in forcing a reappraisal of the contribution of women to literature. But in their search for role models from the past they have tended to favor the writings of the militant, and once more Teasdale's poetry failed to find academic or scholarly supporters. Her unillusioned perception of the position of women in society, carefully masked to suit the conventions of the day, seemed too tame, and her courageous facing of the universal human dilemma, that we are born but to die, seemed not specific enough to the particular issues with which feminists were concerned.

The critical cliché, that lyric poetry defies analysis, has added the final fillip to the critical ignoring of Teasdale's achievement. The limpid surface of her poems projects an air of simplicity and artlessness that is one of the highest forms of art, yet is as difficult to discuss as the songs of Schubert or Brahms.

Teasdale worked within a small compass, dealing with a few themes and a limited range of images; her primary concern was to create unforgettable melodies, a goal that she achieved in a body of work that deserves to be regarded with the best of lyric poetry in English.

Carol B. Schoen

Herbert H. Lehman College
City University of New York

Acknowledgments

I wish to thank the following for permission to quote from manuscripts in their possession: University of Arkansas Library for the letters of John Gould Fletcher; University of Chicago Library for correspondence of Harriet Monroe; Mills Memorial Library of Rollins College for correspondence of Jessie B. Rittenhouse; Houghton Library, Harvard University, for correspondence of Amy Lowell, John Reed, and Witter Bynner; Missouri Historical Society for the correspondence of Sara Teasdale and related papers of Williamina Parrish; Newberry Library, Chicago, for the correspondence of John Myers O'Hara, Marion Cummings, and Eunice Tietjens; Library of Middlebury College for the correspondence of Marguerite Wilkinson; English Poetry Collection in the Special Collections of the Library of Wellesley College for the Rossetti Notebook and the two drafts of *Christina Rossetti, An Intimate Portrait;* Beinecke Rare Book and Manuscript Library of Yale University, Collection of American Literature, for the Travel Diary of Sara Teasdale, 1905, and the Poetry Notebooks of Sara Teasdale, 1911–1932.

"In Florence," "I Am Borne Onward," "Hide and Seek," and "Let Never Music Sound" are reprinted wih permission of Macmillan Publishing Company from *Mirror of the Heart* by Sara Teasdale. Copyright 1984 by Morgan Guaranty Trust Company of New York.

"To Rose" is reprinted with permission of Macmillan Publishing Company from *Rivers to the Sea* by Sara Teasdale. Copyright 1915 by Macmillan Publishing Company, renewed 1943 by Mamie T. Wheless.

"Since There Is No Escape" is reprinted with permission of Macmillan Publishing Company from *Flame and Shadow* by Sara Teasdale. Copyright 1920 by Macmillan Publishing Company, renewed 1948 by Mamie T. Wheless.

"Dedication" is reprinted with permission of Macmillan publishing Company from *Dark of the Moon* by Sara Teasdale. Copyright 1926 by Macmillan Publishing Company, renewed 1954 by Mamie T. Wheless.

Other poems are reprinted with permission of Macmillan Publishing Company from *Collected Poems* by Sara Teasdale. Copyright

Special thanks are due to Leonard Bernstein who encouraged me, read the manuscript, and made invaluable suggestions; to Judith Easton who assisted me in my research; to Cheryl Walker who provided me with her then-unpublished study of Teasdale's poetry. I am most deeply indebted to William Drake, author of *Sara Teasdale, Woman and Poet* and editor of *Mirror of the Heart: Poems of Sara Teasdale,* without whose assistance this project would have been a much poorer effort. He shared with me materials from his own research, made it possible for me to obtain materials from other sources, wrote numerous encouraging letters suggesting areas of research and supplying information from his personal knowledge. In addition, he read the manuscript and offered helpful criticism.

Chronology

1916   Moves to New York City, her permanent residence for the rest of her life.

1917   *The Answering Voice; One Hundred Love Lyrics by Women; Love Songs.*

1918   Columbia Poetry Prize for *Love Songs.*

1919–1920   Santa Barbara, California.

1920   *Flame and Shadow.*

1922   *Rainbow Gold.*

1923   Trip to England with husband.

1924   Trip to France with cousin, Alice Teasdale.

1926   *Dark of the Moon.* Meeting with Margaret Conklin.

1927   Trip to England with Conklin.

1928   Revised edition of *The Answering Voice.*

1929   Reno, Nevada, for divorce.

1930   *Stars Tonight.* Beginning of research on Christina Rossetti.

1931   Trip to England for research on Rossetti.

1932   Trip to England for research on Rossetti. Contracts pneumonia and returns home ill. December, two-week visit to Winter Park, Florida, with Jessie Rittenhouse Scollard.

1933   January 29, found dead of overdose of sleeping pills. October, *Strange Victory* published posthumously.

Chapter One
The Beauty of the Past

Sara Teasdale, in her projected biography of Christina Rossetti, described the period she lived in as "an age of transition."[1] While those words might be applied to any age in human history, Teasdale's observation reflects her perception of her own times and provides a clue to understanding her sense of the world into which she was born and of the myriad of changes that she noted throughout her life. The changes grew out of the contradictory impulses and un-resolved conflicts inherent in the post-Victorian world into which she was born; they assumed overwhelming importance during the post–World War I years of her maturity. She was too intelligent not to be aware of the contradictions, and too honest to dismiss the force of their effects. Out of her attempts to cope with the opposing pulls, she forged her poems and if she was unable to reconcile the oppositions, she was able to find moments of poise, of balance out of which she created lyrics of exquisite beauty.

The city of St. Louis where she was born was itself a city of contradictions. A vast industrial complex whose factories lent a smoky haze to the city and whose waterfront piers and railroad stations provided a key junction between the eastern and western parts of the nation, it sat within the agricultural heart of the Mid-west. One portion of the population had come from the East, bring-ing with them the stern puritan heritage with its emphasis on moral principles and its focus on Heaven or Hell, while a second equally significant group were refugees from Germany who brought with them a love of music and poetry that emphasized the aesthetic aspects of life. Together these groups made St. Louis an intellectual and artistic center, with two universities, a museum and art school, and indoor and outdoor theaters in which were presented grand opera, drama, and concerts.

The fine educational institutions, some founded by the Eliot family, of which T. S. Eliot is the most noted son, looked not to the world around them but to England and Europe for their stimulus and standards, stressing classics that might make a well-educated person feel more at home in the deserted English village described by Oliver Goldsmith than in the small towns of Illinois or Missouri. The plays in the local theaters featured the latest productions of England and Europe, and the museum treasured its French salon paintings. But travel was slow and the culture of the city lagged behind its European and eastern sisters.

Changes also existed in the position of women and were producing irreconcilable contradictions. Although a few brave souls had broken through the conventions and had managed to make careers for themselves, most women accepted their assigned roles as wives and mothers. While the wives and daughters of the more successful businessmen had escaped the drudgery of housework, their husbands treasured the leisure of their women as outward signs of their affluence. Women were still expected to control the domestic management of their homes and professional career aspirations were rarely entertained. Women were expected to be the upholders of the cultural life of the community, to foster music, literature, and arts, but even in these fields it was as amateurs or as appreciators that they were expected to function, not as creators themselves. The Wednesday Club in St. Louis, like many of the women's organizations of the day, held regular meetings at which art, music, and literature were seriously discussed but the women rarely saw themselves as professionals. The club provided an outlet for intellectual pursuits, but not a substitute for their main role as wives and mothers.

Religious beliefs were also in the process of change. The underlying belief in a divinely ordered universe had lost its hold, even while religion maintained its demand for introspection and self-control, and the strictures on behavior were extended to cover the Victorian demand for good manners as if they were aspects of morality, leading to an atmosphere of stifling propriety. Faith in "progress" had been substituted for religion, yet the gross inequities in the society could not always be ignored.

For poets, both men and women, the very standards by which they could judge their creations were in the process of change. The times demanded metrical correctness, elevated diction, the Victorian insistence on moral uplift, a preference for the "ideal" rather than the real, and the worship of the elusive quality called "Beauty." During a period that has been called "the most musically active century in modern times,"[2] the melodic content of poetry had been exalted at the cost of all other values. The result, unfortunately, was to produce delicate sentimental verses that George Santayana was to condemn in *The Genteel Tradition.*

Beset by these contradictions, Sara Teasdale strove to find her own path as a woman and as a poet, to salvage what was valuable to her of the old forms while discarding what was dross; to experiment with the new without destroying the sense of continuity with the past; to balance the safety and security of the traditional woman's role with her ambition and talent as a poet. Teasdale had concluded her description of the transitional nature of Christina Rossetti's world by saying,

We cannot live through one of the crucial acts of the drama of civilization without paying for the privilege. Christina paid heavily, but that is our good fortune, for without conflicting impulses she would not have written poetry. Her method of getting through the ordeal of life was to withdraw into herself and to make her art serve as her solace.[3]

These words apply as well to Sara Teasdale, who, out of the confusions and contradictions of her life and times, drew out the "threads of song."

Chapter Two

The Dreams That Have Gathered in Me

. . . for Sara lived the austere life of a nun, each hour having its fixed and set task—hours of rest, hours of work on her poetry, hours when friends were expected by appointment. . . . So well do I remember being ushered into the large dim parlor . . . by the maid, who would go up and announce my arrival quite as though I were visiting royalty. . . . Sara lived the life of a Princess in her Tower. . . . Nothing was lacking to her except vigorous health.[1]

These words, written by one of Sara Teasdale's closest friends during her years in St. Louis, capture the atmosphere in which Sara Teasdale as woman and poet came to maturity. The particular nature of her life was the result of an amalgam of forces—of the general condition of the late Victorian era, of the special intellectual nature of the midwestern city in which she lived and the particular family of which she was a part. Each contributed a share to the making of the poet—sometimes overlapping in effect to produce exceptional intensity, sometimes contradicting each other to produce insoluble conflict.

Family and Early Years

At the time of Sara's birth, 8 August 1884, her parents were already middle-aged. Her father, at forty-five, was an established, highly respected, and successful businessman who was able to provide his youngest child with the trappings of life that were rare for the average middle-class family. Described as a courtly gentleman, "an elder straight out of the Old Testament, with a long forked beard,"[2] he was the object of deep love and adoration by Sara, who later called him "my first lover."[3] His calm, quiet demeanor contrasted sharply with the bustling, energetic personality of his wife, whose domineering ways often conflicted with the child's emerging

4

personality. Both parents came from families that had settled in America early in its history, the father's family arriving in 1792, the mother's in 1634. Not only were there, among their forebears, many successful businessmen and educators, but there was also more than a sprinkling of religious leaders. Both parents were devout Baptists with a strong puritanical streak who had first met at church and continued to be churchgoers throughout their lives. The family into which Sara was born already included two sons, aged fourteen and nineteen, and a daughter, aged seventeen.

The combination of the comparative wealth and their age probably contributed to the overindulgent and overprotective manner with which they treated this late-born child. On a psychological level, the mother's extreme protectiveness may have been, as William Drake, Sara Teasdale's biographer, has suggested, "an expression of guilt and resentment against this offspring whose birth embarrassed her as a kind of sexual indiscretion, a hostility veiled by a cloud of parental overconcern."[4] Named Sarah Trevor and called "Sadie" by her family, she was granted every luxury and, unlike most girls of her generation, was never expected to perform any domestic chores. But growing up in a household of adults, she had few companions of her own age and was expected to curb her naturally exuberant nature and behave in a placid, obedient manner to suit the demands of the more mature members of the household. Two photographs of her as a child present these contrasting sides of her personality; in one she sits docilely on a bench holding a doll in one hand and a large garden hat in the other, her hair neatly arranged in curls, a sweet, serene expression on her face; in the other she stands, slightly pigeon-toed, her hair tousled, her eyes wide and questioning, her lips pursed in anger, and her small fist clenched at her side.[5] This divided self, perceived in many different ways throughout her life, was both a source of her troubles and her impulse to poetry. She seems to have spent much of her time in the prim daintiness of her room, in a world of daydreams, inventing stories to stave off the loneliness and fears that seemed to threaten to engulf her.

One long-lasting effect of these early years was a morbid concern for her physical well-being. She was considered to be frail and to suffer from frequent respiratory infections. Then, too, Sara's mother had been sickly as a child and her treatment of her youngest daughter may have echoed the treatment she had received. In addition, sickliness was, during the Victorian era, often regarded as a sign of

gentility and Sara's frailty may have been accepted as an indication
of the family's social status. Consequently, each cold was treated as
if it were incipient pneumonia, and careful control was imposed on
her daily schedule to ensure that she had sufficient rest.

Her health was considered to be so delicate that even her education
was restricted. Until she was nine years old, she was tutored at
home, mostly by her sister Mamie, who not only served as a younger
surrogate mother, but who also was responsible for fostering the
child's interest in literature and budding appreciation of beauty. Of
the numerous stories and poems she read to her younger sister, "A
Christmas Carol" by Christina Rossetti and the music of its closing
lines, "Snow had fallen, Snow on snow, / Snow on Snow / In the
bleak midwinter / Long ago," so appealed to the child that she
recited it for hours after, dancing to its rhythms and remembering
the incident for the rest of her life. While the story is charming in
its own right, it is repeated here to accentuate the profound effect
that the music of poetry had for her even at this early age. She
invariably referred to her work as "songs" and many years later she
was to talk of the "magic of melody," this primitive, mystical level
surpassing all other values of poetry for her throughout her life.

The schools Teasdale attended provided a solid base of knowledge
with a strong emphasis on the classics of English literature. Students
were taught also to be aware of the world around them, to recognize
and to name the flowers and the stars, an ability Teasdale preserved
throughout her life. One friend of later days wrote: "she always
talked concretely, of the wild plants by the stream bank which she
knew by name everyone, of the lake and its various personalities,
'the unchanging, everchanging sea,' or of the stars which were all
individual friends of hers."[6] Orderly habits were instilled, such as
the listing of all books read, which she did until the last years of
her life, the recording of the final version of her poems in small red
notebooks, and carefully indicating when and where they were published. The early notebooks do not survive, but those from 1911
on are still available. She seems not to have been a particularly
outstanding scholar, and while her literary talents were recognized
by her teachers, Sara's later memories of her writings during these
years seem confined to some translations of Heine, a few verses
written after an unhappy attraction to a young person, and numerous
parodies and attempts at humor. The request that she read her poems

at her graduation from Hosmer Hall School in 1903 was turned down and although she did write the school song, the result does not survive. The entries in the reading notebook begin with such books as Louisa May Alcott's *Little Women* and Lewis Carroll's *Alice in Wonderland,* but soon branch out to include, while she was still in her early teens, an extraordinary range from Ruskin's *Sesame and Lilies* to Bunyan's *Pilgrim's Progress,* but center heavily on the romantic novels of Sir Walter Scott and other nineteenth-century authors. Since her reading notebook is confined to "titles of only those books I have read from cover to cover"[7] as she wrote on the inside front cover of her notebook, it does not include many of the poets who were influential in her development, notably Elizabeth Barrett Browning and Christina Rossetti (these she probably found in anthologies, such as Edmund Clarence Stedman's *A Victorian Anthology* and *An American Anthology*), nor does it include her readings in the Bible, parts of which she is known to have read and reread.

The photographs of Teasdale as a young woman show her to be pleasant looking, although not pretty, of medium height but with an extremely slender build; she had a mane of auburn hair, striking blue eyes, and a wide mouth. What they do not show are eyeglasses, which must have given her a schoolteacherish look, a constant reminder of what Dorothy Parker was to note a few years later: "Men seldom make passes at girls who wear glasses." Although the eyes look out seriously, a slight smile plays along the lips, suggesting again the duality in her nature. In her home she was considered quiet, and to strangers she seemed shy, yet her friends remembered her witty good humor and bursts of enthusiasm.[8] Puritan standards and Victorian codes of behavior dominated her upbringing, but her romantic nature and her interest in love were so strong that she once constructed a shrine to Aphrodite in her bedroom.[9] In later years she was to describe herself as a combination of Pagan and Puritan or Spartan and Sybarite. The regime imposed upon her because of her frail health caused her to spend many hours in solitude, missing out on the usual outings and parties enjoyed by her contemporaries, yet she longed for friends and developed a crush on a young man whom she only saw from her window. The extreme orderliness of her life contrasted with her sensuous love of light, color, and particularly music.

Europe and the Middle East

A significant opportunity to broaden her horizons and to indulge this love of the sensuous came when she accompanied her mother on a five-month trip to the Middle East and Europe in 1905. Many of the places chosen to visit probably reflected the mother's religious interest in the lands of the Bible—the Holy Land and Egypt—but the pair also stopped in Spain and Athens before, and went on to Rome, Paris, and London after. In Teasdale's journal, schoolgirlish in tone and full of superlatives, she recorded her impressions of the places and people she met. Perhaps the most long-lasting result of the trip for her development as a poet is her reaction to the first sight of the ocean. She had spent most of her summers at the family's country estate in Charlevoix, a summer community on the shores of Lake Michigan, so she was accustomed to large bodies of water, but she was not prepared for the overwhelming response to the ocean. In the journal she wrote:

The blue of the ocean is deeper than that of Lake Michigan, I think— more of a peacock blue and far more magnificent, for the waves are veritable mountains. You can have no idea of the sea until you are in the midst of it. I have never seen a marine picture that gave a real idea of it. It is more restless, passionate and powerful than any painting can be. The foam on the great waves that break upon the ship is like lace laid over sea-foam green satin, only how *much* more beautiful! The foam goes in myriads of little half ovals and covers the whole of the broken waves with its network. . . .[10]

Its appeal was religious as well as sensuous, for she also wrote, "The ocean would be a fine place to convert people, for you can't help thinking of your spiritual condition." Throughout her life the image of the sea would be one of the most potent symbols, in part because of its ability to combine these disparate elements in her nature.

While the ocean compelled her attention during the voyage over, it was the colors in the art and architecture, the literary allusions, and music that captured her attention in Europe. The sensuous hues of the stained glass windows of the great cathedrals of Seville and of the Murillo paintings overwhelmed her, as did the gardens of the Alcazar—"Seville is fairyland," she wrote. In Paris she was struck by the light-colored stone of the houses, the glass in Ste. Chapelle, "—as tho' they were made of rubies, emeralds, sapphires, and amethysts." Even the setting for "the most beautiful thing in the world—the Venus de Milo," against a dark red curtain—appealed to her. The literary influences on her are apparent from her entries. Some paintings in the Louvre reminded her of Keats and Shelley, whose graves she had visited in Rome; the Italian landscape brought back thoughts of Robert Browning. In London she searched out Swinburne's home in Putney, and Elizabeth Barrett's home at 50 Wimpole Street, as well as visiting Shakespeare's home in Stratford. Special trips were made to hear the works of Bach and a highlight of the journey was the chance to hear Wagner's *Tristan und Isolde.* Although she had been plagued during the trip with several bouts of poor health that limited her time in Athens and had been depressed by the poverty and filth in the Holy Land, the trip introduced her to visions of beauty she had till then only dreamed or read about.

The Potters and the *Potters Wheel*

Teasdale's decision to make a serious commitment to writing probably stems from her association with a group of young women whom she had met after graduation and who from 1903 to 1907 joined together to form a group known as the Potters. Among other activities, they produced a monthly magazine, the *Potters Wheel.* It is instructive to study this association not simply for the light it sheds on the development of Teasdale's talent, but also for what it says about avenues available to talented young women at that time. The eight who were involved were all interested in the various arts— literature, sculpture, music, acting, painting, and photography— as well as science. Williamina Parrish, the driving force of the group, who could "produce a superior watercolor, write a creditable sonnet, take a leading part in a play and carry it off to perfection,"[11] was particularly noted as a photographer whose work later appeared in numerous camera magazines. Like most apprentice artists, these women showed brief flashes of talent and, given a more disciplined environment, might have matured more fully, yet they saw no better outlet for their skills than this seriously amateur fashion. College and art school were available for women at that time, and two of the group did attend, but it took special courage to do so, for the medical opinion from no less eminent a source than Dr. Clarke of

Harvard stated that women "were destroying their wombs by pursuing higher education intended only for men."[12]

The organization founded by these young women was part of a pattern of women's intellectual activities that had been developing through the latter part of the nineteenth century. The particular group after which they modeled themselves was the Wednesday Club in St. Louis, organized in 1887 and devoted to discussing and fostering the arts. These clubs, by their very existence, suggest that women of intellectual pretensions were aware of the double bind they had been placed in by their society: on the one hand, they were reared to be the protectors of the culture, to cultivate their own artistic sensibilities and to devote their energies at least in part to those pursuits, but on the other hand, they found that the only place for these cultivated talents in the society to which they belonged was on a part-time, nonprofessional basis. Their domestic duties and the strictures placed on possible careers for middle-class women effectively limited them. They might dabble in the arts themselves, but even then critical appraisal was usually less stringent than that meted out to men. Teaching as a career for women had undergone a substantial increase during this period, but the difficulty of combining marriage and career was underscored by the image of the spinster schoolteacher. Marriage, home, and family were the accepted goals for young women.

In some ways, the situation for women of Teasdale's generation was even more difficult than that of earlier generations, as Elaine Showalter[13] and Cheryl Walker[14] have pointed out. Whereas women in the mid–nineteenth century could decide to be career women and forgo thoughts of marriage and family, by the 1880s the image of the New Woman had been presented, a woman who could expect to combine both career and family responsibilities. The difficulty of such a life is amply discussed by the women themselves, some of them the same age as Teasdale, in the articles published by the *Nation* in 1926 and 1927 that Showalter reprints. But the inspiration for their effort effectively summarized by Dorothy Bromley in "Feminist—New Style"[15] continued to influence popular opinion and called for a "well-balanced" life that combined work and love. With "more freedom and honesty within the marriage relation," women would, Bromley claimed, be able to develop their own work interests. Instead of presenting women with clear-cut choices, it left them with a hazy promise that all things were possible.

Rebelliousness specifically against Victorian restrictions on women is perhaps too strong a word to use to describe the attitude of the women who formed the Potters; yet to examine their activities without sensing the spirit of protest that lurked behind them would be to miss much of the significance of their efforts. They dressed up for their meetings, not in finery, as their mothers did, but as characters from *Alice in Wonderland,* as visitors to Beethoven, as children from literary works or "grubby chimney sweeps." In place of the propriety that governed social events of their time, their meetings were characterized as "sitting on the floor, occasionally drinking wine by the light of an alcohol lamp," their talk a "regular simultaneous-combustion conversation" unbound by the "mortal coils of convention and politeness."[16]

The level of knowledge of the group was high, reflecting the excellent high school preparation they had had in most of the classics of Western thought. But, in addition, they showed an awareness of the new antimodernist currents of the time, which were, as Jackson Lears has pointed out, attempts to cope with the social and cultural issues of the day.[17] Lears mentions the strong interest in medievalism, which he regards as an attempt to return to the childhood of the world when people were "able to experience ecstasy and spontaneous feeling," unlike the control expected from the current society. The lives of saints and religious figures presented a picture of "simple faith unhampered by learning," while the fondness for myth provided an escape from the demands for rationalism and a rekindled sense of awe and dread. Medieval characters were seen as vital, enjoying a gaiety that made life one of carnival exuberance. The medieval cathedral became a symbol of the autonomous impulse toward art and of vital communal activity. "In the cultural criticism of the turn of the century, saints and cathedral builders emerged to rebuke ethical confusion and to dissipate an enveloping feeling of impotence."[18] For the Potters, this concern found expression in tales and drawings of knights and ladies, in the frequent use of stained glass in their artwork. For Teasdale, its appeal found expression in a concentrated reading of certain legends. She read versions of Tristan and Isolde by Belloc, Swinburne, and Wagner, as well as those by such less well known writers as Joseph Bédier, Martha Austin, and Basil Crump. The story of Francesca and Paolo shows up in her reading notebook in works by Shelley, D'Annunzio, Leigh Hunt, Stephen Phillips, George Boker, and even Dante. And for the romance of Guenevere, she read Tennyson, William Morris, and especially Richard Hovey, whose blank-verse plays she returned to again and again.

Another aspect of the new thought that appealed to these young women was the arts and crafts movement. Based in part on Tolstoy's notion of the return to the "simple life" and the work of William Morris, it had had a significant element of social criticism in Europe but not in the American version, which tended to emphasize the spirit of human creativity, of promoting standards of aestheticism in daily life, of ending the "crinkum-crankum of Victorian taste," and of "encourag[ing] a more open admiration for aesthetic activity as an end in itself."[19] The kinds of artwork that these young women undertook included designs for wallpaper, fabrics, lamp shades, fans, and stained glass windows. Chief among its values for them was its demand for discipline in creative efforts and its insistence on the importance of craftsmanship. The very name they gave to themselves emphasized this notion of creativity. The most obvious connection to the movement was their publication, the *Potters Wheel,* a completely handcrafted book with all original artwork, all hand-lettered written material, frequently in carefully interlaced lettering or in a style to echo old manuscripts. Even the binding was done by hand. Only one copy of the magazine was produced each month.

Perhaps the most significant element in their activities for Teasdale was the way she used these interests to focus on issues that concerned women, especially women who through achievement or position represented leadership. It was, it seems, an effort to find a "usable past" for herself outside the patriarchal structure. She was strongly influenced by the fragments of Sappho, whose work was extremely popular in the nineteenth century as a symbol of burning passion, but for Teasdale she was also a symbol of a creator of beauty and poetry. In their delving into medieval legend it was the lives of the women that concerned her most completely—Guenevere rather than Arthur, Iseult instead of Tristan, Francesca, not Paolo. As a group, the Potters delighted in the work of Fiona MacLeod, whose writings they mistakenly believed to be by a woman from the period known as the Celtic Twilight, but which in fact had been written by the nineteenth-century William Sharpe. But their susceptibility to fakes only underlines their rebellion against the existing mores.

One group of women who particularly attracted the Potters were the famous actresses of the day, some of whom had appeared in St.

Louis. These actresses—Julia Marlowe, Olga Nethersole, Maude Adams, Nazimova, and Eleonora Duse—filled a special niche whose appeal was based, first, on the fact that as artists, they translated the beauties of the plays in which they appeared with such intensity that often the distinction between the actress and her role was blurred. These actresses also served the function of becoming themselves an object of art, fulfilling Walter Pater's injunction "to make of one's life a work of art." Teasdale's personal obsession was with Duse. She never saw her act, however, despite the fact that she was appearing in Paris while Teasdale was there. In addition to her fame as an actress, Duse was appealing as a person not only for her physical beauty but also for the passion of her love affair with the playwright D'Annunzio.

If there is any unity behind all these figures, it is the combination of their beauty, their passion, and their tragedies as victims of love. For Teasdale these women were joined by the Pre-Raphaelite ladies, the Greek statue of Venus, and especially the character of Helen of Troy. Yet she maintained, as well, a deep attraction for chaste innocent figures such as the princesses in the tower that dot the Arthurian legends. This contradiction reflects the confusion of her society, which idealized the chaste woman and which was only beginning to accept the notion of female sexual passion. Earlier in the nineteenth century middle-class women were believed to be asexual, concerned only with having children and pleasing their husbands. By midcentury, however, the literature by both men and women was filled with images of passionate women. For women like Teasdale and her friends, who were interested in becoming writers, there was a dilemma summed up by Ellen Moers:

In no area of literature have women writers been subjected to such earnest, constant, and contradictory advice as in the literature of love. Women are the passionate sex, they are told, and therefore love is their natural subject; but they must not write about it. If they avoid love, that proves they are mere women, inferior to men, next to whom women are always told they are cold, narrow, childish. If they dwell on love they are doing what is expected of the worst of women, who are said to be stupid, sentimental, hysterical creatures incapable of thinking of anything else.[20]

One American poet, Ella Wheeler Wilcox, "created a scandal and became a sensation"[21] when she dared to publish a volume entitled *Poems of Passion* in 1883 despite her very decorous personal life.

The issue was still primarily an artistic one for the Potters, whose experience with men outside their families was minimal or non-existent. Instead, they focused their romantic thoughts on each other, developed crushes, wrote poetry to each other. This behavior is explained by Lillian Faderman, who has examined women's relationships with women as early as the sixteenth century and describes the closeness that women in the mid–nineteenth century felt for each other. After discussing the "separate spheres" of men and women demanded by the culture, she goes on to write:

Since middle and upper-class women were separated from men not only in their daily occupations, but in their spiritual and leisure interests as well, outside of the practical necessities of raising a family there was little that tied the sexes together. But with other females a woman inhabited the same sphere, and she could be entirely trusting and unrestrained. She could share sentiment, her heart—all emotions that manly males had to repress in favor of "rationality"—with another female. And regardless of the intensity of the feeling that might develop between them, they need not attribute it to the demon, sexuality, since women supposedly had none. They could safely see it as an effusion of the spirit. The shield of passionlessness that a woman was trained to raise before a man could be lowered with another woman without fear of losing her chastity and reputation and health.[22]

For Teasdale, the meetings of the Potters provided a circle of friends who were interested in similar pursuits, who could be both supportive and critical of her writing. Within the group she could let loose the exuberant spirits that were so restricted within her home. She was noted in the group for her sense of humor and is remembered as "overflowing with high spirits, fun and a keen interest in everything."[23] When the group went on an outing to an old farmhouse outside St. Louis known as Saxton's, Teasdale joined them for full days of roaming the fields and woods, returning to their Spartan living quarters late in the evening, despite her fears of illness.

In 1906 some issues of *Potters Wheel* were brought to the attention of William Reedy, the editor of a weekly newspaper in St. Louis, the *Mirror,* which had achieved a national reputation through its editor's wide-ranging interests in avant-garde literature and thought. In its pages were published the works of Baudelaire, Shaw, Yeats, Synge, Sandburg, Lindsay, and Millay. And he was also responsible for encouraging young talent such as Fannie Hurst, Orrick Johns, Zoë Akins, and Marianne Moore, all from St. Louis, as well as providing the germ of the idea for the *Spoon River Anthology* to Edgar Lee Masters. Reedy selected a prose sketch by Teasdale for publication.

The sketch describes in pseudomythic language, with the simplicity of a refined incantatory style, a woman totally the opposite of the Victorian ideal and especially of Teasdale herself.[24] The woman of the story is extraordinarily beautiful, almost an enchantress in her power to command a man's attention. With insolent disregard of the man's interest, she takes the miraculous crystal cup he offers her, drains the wine which her admirer has lovingly gathered over a long period of time, and places the cup on a stone wall so carelessly that it shatters into a thousand pieces. She then leaves the man, thus providing an image of a woman whose arrogant use of power to satisfy only herself thoroughly disregards the man's needs, hopes, and desires. The sensuous details—honey-sweet grapes, hair like "gold that goldsmiths had worked over lovingly"—combined with the cold disdain of the goddesslike woman present an image of defiance to Victorian standards for a woman in love who is supposed to be submissive and self-sacrificing.

Reedy's publication of this sketch and of another poem provided the impetus Teasdale needed to prepare a volume of poems, and in 1907 the Poet Lore Company agreed to bring out the book if she would assume the expense of printing. Her indulgent parents supplied the funds, and in September 1907 *Sonnets to Duse and Other Poems* appeared. The poems represented a careful culling of the work she had written for the *Potters Wheel* and had been assembled under the critical eye of Williamina Parrish, who was, at that time, her "literary confessor." The fact that only nine of the twenty-nine poems of this early work were included in the *Collected Poems,* which Teasdale selected, provides an inkling of her later evaluation of these early efforts.

For modern readers, accustomed to the free forms and unrestricted emotional range of poetry today, these works may seem tame and rigid, yet are genuine flashes of poetic talent, a sure sense of craft developed over years of disciplined work, and an attempt to face issues and problems that were significant in the lives of women at that time. The poems were, as a group, as one critic described them, "what any well-read, intelligent, thoughtful young girl would produce";[25] nevertheless, they reveal a talent for musical patterns, a developing craftsmanship, a sense of the need to discipline experience to the demands of art. They represented what Teasdale later said of Christina Rossetti's early work: "She had learned that through poetry she could say concisely what she wanted to say."[26] Later she would learn, as she had added about Rossetti, to "say what she had never dreamed of saying."

In creating her poems, Teasdale was attempting to capture the elusive quality called beauty, which had been the goal of much nineteenth-century art. Always hazy in its definition, it included in its meaning some sense of a transcendent reality that Keats implied in his "Beauty is truth, truth beauty," and it owed much to Walter Pater's dictum. Beauty had something of the quality of ecstatic revelation and was worshipped with the same zeal that had once belonged to religion. In Teasdale's early groping toward understanding and re-creating this beauty, she seems to have envisaged it as in some way juxtaposing opposites—song and silence, pain and pleasure—in a fleeting moment, like a verbal snapshot. The polarity of her thinking, a heritage from her puritan background, which saw the world in terms of good and evil, saved and damned, black and white, and eliminated all shades of gray between, dominated her vision of the world. To perceive beauty meant, for Teasdale, the awareness of the coexistence of these opposing forces.

Poetry could serve that beauty by presenting these opposing forces not as clashing but in some sort of harmony. And that harmony could be found in the music of the poem itself. The particular melodic quality that Teasdale strove to achieve in her poems is less noticeable today than in her time. In the nineteenth century the relationship between poetry and music was extremely close.[27] Tennyson is said to have so accentuated the music of his verse that when he read it the meaning of the words was nearly lost. The importance of music in poetry is never ignored by critics, but few have captured its deeper significance better than Hugh Kenner:

You've surely at some time or other tried to reconstruct the words of a familiar song, only to discover for the first time that you had no idea what some of them were. You'll search your memory in vain. Whole phrases aren't there; you literally never heard them. They were masked by the piano or by slurred intonation. And yet you had the illusion of total lucidity. So how did you follow the song when you were hearing it?

As you listened, you relied on a pattern the music sustains: a pattern of intonations, pitches and pauses, with no inherent semantic content at all. This pattern locates key phrases; it holds them in relation amid ascents and descents of key, amid instances of urgency and linger; and it lets you imagine you've discerned what came between. The structure of meaning is a kind of rhythmic envelope within which we connect the dots between perceived words. We do this without knowing we do it. Poets know about it and know we do it. It's a skill of ours they can count on.[28]

The music of poetry was basic for Teasdale; she always referred to her work as "songs," even to the extent of singing her own poems to herself or making up a tune to fit the words of others. The poets she most loved were known for their melodic lines, especially Rossetti and Swinburne, and even when she could appreciate the values in a poet such as Robert Browning, she rankled at the harshness of his phrasing. She could also value Swinburne for his irreverent attitude toward Victorian conventions, which she could understand even if she was too bound to them to discard them completely. His love of music and his distaste for Victorian hypocrisy were significant factors in Teasdale's own poetic development.

The opening section of *Sonnets to Duse* is devoted to nine worshipful poems to Duse, eight of them sonnets, interspersed with reproductions of photographs of the actress. Three of the poems are about Duse in the character of Anna in D'Annunzio's *The Dead City*. In this lurid drama of incest, adulterous love, and murder, Duse's character is a blind woman of ancient Greece who must listen to the other characters' confessions and endure the knowledge of the part she had inadvertently played in causing their tragedies. For Teasdale, she is a symbol of all the beauties of the ancient world, of its architecture, of the Homeric legends and Greek tragedies, of Venus and of Sappho. Three other poems are to the actress in the role of Francesca da Rimini, also a play by D'Annunzio, retelling the medieval story of the woman who refused to marry the man her father had chosen, who ran away with her lover Paolo and was captured and executed. The photograph shows her to be like a Pre-Raphaelite painting of a flowerlike woman, and in the poem the connection to flowers is also stressed. The second sonnet emphasizes Francesca's bloody end. The remaining sonnets address Duse directly, two focusing on the beauty of her face while the third speaks of her melodious voice, which the poet connects to Sicilian shepherds, Egyptian kings, and Orpheus. All the poems are totally adoring, as if addressed to a goddess.

The choice of Duse as the subject for so many poems raises the question of what meaning this cosmopolitan actress may have had for the provincial American girl. There is, of course, the obvious appeal of the exotic, but, in addition, she represented a woman who sought for and achieved fame as a leader in her profession. Both in her personal life and in the roles she played, she exemplified the woman of passion who refused to hide her emotions behind the mask of convention; equally important, she was an artist in whom the key elements of love and beauty were combined. But it certainly was not as a role model that Teasdale and her friends admired her; her break with the moral standards of the day was beyond the scope of anything but their fantasy life. Probably, however, for Teasdale Duse provided a feminine equivalent of a muse—that imaginary creature who, like a mother, feeds the creative process and, like a lover, provides an erotic impulse. The muse is an image of power and the idea that it should be a female for women has raised questions among modern feminist critics. [29] But as Adrienne Rich has pointed out, women writers need "a female precursor who . . . provides by example that a revolt against patriarchal literary authority is possible." [30] Teasdale and her friends found in actresses like Duse not simply literary models but also figures whose actions could justify their own efforts at self-definition.

The second half of the volume contains short lyrics on a variety of subjects—one on a Japanese incense burner, inspired by her reading of Lafcadio Hearn, three children's poems that owe much to her familiarity with Robert Louis Stevenson, two poems to Sappho, a sonnet to a schoolteacher friend of the Potters, and several love poems. Most of the poems are the wistful apostrophes to love and beauty by an inexperienced girl whose mind has been influenced by romantic literature, yet beneath the surface occasionally lie thoughts and ideas of much sterner stuff.

One of the concerns that Teasdale deals with in the *Sonnets to Duse* is the position of women. It is at once apparent from the subject of many of the poems that she is focusing on women of strength and power whom she admires and seeks to emulate although they were hardly the image her family or culture might have thought proper. The sonnets to Duse herself praise her for her ability to convey the music from the past to the present generation and for her beauty, which is so great it will survive even death itself. As a character in the play *Francesca da Rimini,* she is presented as a woman who openly acknowledged her passionate nature and accepted the penalty that would follow. Despite the obvious sinfulness of Francesca's actions and the widely known immorality of Duse's liaison with the author Gilbert D'Annunzio, the poet dreams that she would be "her guardian angel." In every case, however, the woman is seen as suffering, her pain apparently a necessary corollary to her beauty.

Other images of strong women appear in the book. The "Sonnet to L. R. E." is a tribute to Lillie Rose Ernst, a teacher who was an adviser to the Potters and a significant leader in public education. The great Greek poet Sappho is the subject of two poems and in each her passion and her genius, "sole perfect singer that the world has heard," are reasons for admiration. Even the image of women that comes through one of the lyrics suggests Teasdale's admiration of power. In "Roses and Rue" the poet-narrator tells of having at some earlier time chosen "laurel," the symbol of fame and accomplishment, rather than "roses," the symbol of love, but now that she wants affection it is too late; all that is available is "rue," the emblem of regret. It is important to note here that the narrator has chosen to be a person of achievement, rather than vice versa.

Such poems might not seem particularly bold to today's women, yet they need to be looked at from the vantage point of Teasdale's world. They avoided the trap of much women's poetry at that time of purely sentimental or decorative verse, the "literary embroidery" that Genevieve Taggard eschewed for herself;[31] they considered significant themes of the right to achievement and power. They acknowledged the facts of women's life with its unavoidable suffering but presented women as passionate creatures with a right to their own emotion.

Moderate as it may seem to modern eyes, the defiance—that would choose the laurel of fame even if it cost the roses of love, that would regard the image of the Duse and the "fallen women" she portrayed as a guardian angel, "a sister to the noblest that we know"—is captured in another way in the sonnet "To Joy" with its irreverent attitude toward religion:

> Lo, I am happy, for my eyes have seen
> Joy glowing here before me, face to face;
> His wings were arched above me for a space,

> I kissed his lips, no bitter came between.
> The air is vibrant where his feet have been,
> And full of song and color is his place.
> His wondrous presence shed about a grace
> That lifts and hallows all that once was mean.
> I may not sorrow for I saw the light,
> Tho' I shall walk in valley ways for long,
> I still shall hear the echo of the song,—
> My life is measured by its one great height.
> Joy holds more grace than pain can ever give,
> And by my glimpse of joy my soul shall live.
>
> (*CP,* 5)

It is a curious poem, for while it celebrates the transcendent quality of pure happiness, it does so in language that often suggests religious consolation, which, for Teasdale's family as devout Baptists, was usually regarded as available in Heaven to those who accepted the pain and denial of life. Not only does she use words such as *grace* and *hallows,* but the line "Tho' I shall walk in valley ways for long" echoes the twenty-third Psalm, the one most frequently used for funerals, praising the endurance of pain and suffering as a testament to faith in God's reward. Even the opening ". . . for my eyes have seen . . ." is reminiscent both in its rhythm and its language of the opening of Julia Ward Howe's "Battle Hymn of the Republic," the second line of which speaks of "the coming of the Lord." The "Lord" that Teasdale presents, however, is a personification of pleasure and his presence is described in sensuous detail—it glows, it is vibrant, "full of song and color." The values usually given to the deity are here usurped by earthly happiness— "And by my glimpse of joy my soul shall live." The very musicality of the poem with its frequent triplet rhythm captures the spirit of enthusiasm for life. Her technical skill in manipulating the words helps stress these points. In the second line the juxtaposition of "Joy glowing here" effectively slows down the pace, forcing the reader to give equal accent to "joy" and "glow" and prominence to the fact that it is "here"—not hereafter—that the value of living can be found.

The only other poem in the collection that specifically refers to God in ways appropriate to the Christian deity is "Dead Love" and it offers more a sense of bewilderment at his purposes than any reverence. The poem tells of a lover who has died and whom God

"Took . . . to a Silent Land." The narrator responds, "I cannot weep, I cannot pray. . . . I only watch how God gives love. And then leaves lovers all alone." In other poems where a reader might expect a mention of God, some other word is substituted: in the "Sonnet to L. R. E." power is attributed to "The Poet"; in "Triolets" the poet prays to Aphrodite.

The courage to speak out so freely was not, however, so easily obtained and one of the most frequent themes that underly these poems is the struggle between "song," Teasdale's word for her poetry, and "silence." In some measure this had been a frequent problem for women. The propriety of not airing one's emotions in public had caused Caroline Gilman, sixty years earlier, to worry through sleepless nights about the publication of her poem: "as alarmed as if I had been detected in man's apparel,"[33] and Emily Dickinson in poem 1129 recognized the danger when she advised "tell all the truth but tell it slant."

Teasdale's confusion over her right to be a writer, much less a poet, reflects what Gilbert and Grubar have called women's "anxiety of authorship."[33] Tracing through centuries of women's writing, they see the right to authorship as a dominant concern. To the "dread" of the antagonism of male readers, Teasdale's culturally conditioned timidity about self-dramatization, her dread of the patriarchal authority over art, her anxiety about the impropriety of "female invention" that they mention, can be added, in these poems, a desire not to appear to be complaining. It is as if the opposite of speech were, for her, a revelation of complaint or self-pity. For Teasdale there may have been a personal problem related to her family. Will Parrish quotes her as saying, "Here is Miss Sadie whining again"[34] when she read her published poems. The implication is that someone in her family had used such terms in talking about her, causing an inhibition.

Teasdale used a number of devices that would permit her to speak her thoughts without overstepping the boundaries as she perceived them. By expressing her thoughts as tributes to Duse not as she was as a person but as she appeared in photographs, frequently photographs that showed her portraying roles of legendary women, Teasdale established a significant distance between herself and the emotions she wished to convey. The use of traditional meters and forms also provided a distancing effect, for her verse then might seem to be ballads from an ancient time, for instance, or a mere playing with accepted emotions within a conventional form.

The use of traditional meters and forms was valuable not only as a distancing technique, but also because it declared an intention to be considered a serious poet, not simply an amateur. Much of the poetry by women was given second-class status by male critics and Suzanne Juhasz[35] has amplified this issue by explaining one of the problems women poets faced prior to the modern period: women whose poetry failed to show knowledge of poetic traditions were held in contempt although few women had the time or access to study those forms. Teasdale was fortunate that she did have the time and that her education and her own studies had provided just such knowledge; by her use of a broad range of historical events and of a variety of traditional verse-forms, she was asking for the critical attention reserved for the best poets. She even went so far as to use the far more difficult Petrarchan form of the sonnet rather than the Shakespearean form to underscore her determination. For her lyrics she experimented with triolets, French verse forms, and ballad stanzas. Free-verse forms had not yet been explored to any extent so she could not have been expected to employ them. The use of a variety of these traditional forms declared that she not only wanted to speak out, but that she wanted to be heard by the best listeners, even while it provided the cloak to mask the emotions she wanted to express.

Teasdale's conflict over her right to speak, nevertheless, persisted even within those constraints. In the *Sonnets to Duse* the overriding value is given to silence. In one, the "mouth's mute weariness" is praised to the extent that "God loves its silence better than a prayer." In another, it is "in the silence of your lifted face" that "vanished Grecian beauty lives again." The silence of Duse in the face of pain has enhanced her beauty, and the poet says, "Tho' your woes increase, The gods shall hear no crying for release. . . ." Yet there is value to speech and "song." The music of Duse's voice re-creates the music of the ancient world, and if she should speak to Venus she, too, will find a voice. Sappho's poems are approved of because they are "like sparks that tell the glory of a flame" and "living still, they sting us into tears."

Sometimes the problem of song versus silence merges into the question of the proper stance for a woman. In "The Meeting" the proper Victorian child-woman in her exclaims, "I'm happy, I'm happy. I saw my love today," but because of this propriety she is too shy to speak to him. One poem, which appears to present an overly submissive woman, however, conceals an ambiguous message. "The Gift" begins by asking "What can I give you, my lord, my lover, / You who have given the world to me," and closes with the answer, "I bid you awake at dawn and discover / I have gone my way and left you free." The self-abnegation that is suggested is, however, undercut by the middle stanza:

> All that I have are gifts of your giving—
> If I gave them again, you would find them old,
> And your soul would weary of always living
> Before the mirror my life would hold.
>
> (*CP,* 5)

What seems to be suggested here is that if women were as uncreative and as thoroughly dependent on men as Victorian myth would have it, then men could not help but be bored by them. The decision to leave, rather than being a submissive act, is actually quite an assertive one, for it is the woman who has taken control of the situation, not the man.

But the poems that most reflect Teasdale's life up to this point are the group that seem rooted in a world of dreams. Although the Potters group provided Teasdale with a valuable social and intellectual outlet, she spent endless hours alone. Much of the time she was confined by the innumerable respiratory ailments and digestive problems that continued to plague her and that seemed to grow worse as she matured. And other hours of quiet were enforced in an effort to stave off further sickness. During these periods she dwelt in a world of her own creations. When she emerged into the "real world" she could not help but be struck by the contrast between it and her life of dreams. This contrast is caught by two of the poems in which the narrator is imagined to be a child, reflecting the influence of Robert Louis Stevenson. In "Wishes" she captures with remarkable awareness the child's immersion in magical fantasy, the belief that wishes can influence reality. The child wishes for a cat and dawdles when she takes a walk, fully expecting to find one on the street. Her nurse, unaware of the child's fantasy, impatiently urges her to stop staring and walk along. In another fantasy the child wishing for a balloon expects to find it by the clock at home, only to be disappointed. Unfortunately, the last stanza diminishes the wonder and mystery of the child's thoughts and the pain of disappointment that Teasdale had so successfully captured, by a pious message that wishes are fun even though they don't come true. In "Dusk in Autumn" the child sees from her window witches having a party and wishes she might be invited.

The contrast between dream world and reality finds more mature expression in the sonnet that describes, in sensuous detail, the beauty of a ship sailing in the sunset only to show the same ship in a gray dawn looking dull and faded. The image is likened to a woman she loved who once seemed beautiful and now seems plain without the magic of the sunset's light.

"The House of Dreams" captures best of all the pain of discovering that reality is harsher than dreams. While it is true, as William Drake has suggested, that it had sprung from her "crippling childhood" during which "she had been kept a child, deprived of the strength and self-sufficiency to make an independent life for herself, or even to cope with the emotions she summoned up,"[36] the poem speaks to all who have discovered how little the real world conforms to our hopes and expectations:

> I built a little House of Dreams
>   And fenced it all about,
> But still I heard the Wind of Truth
>   That roared without.
>
> I laid a fire of Memories
>   And sat before the glow,
> But through the chinks and round the door
>   The wind would blow.
>
> I left the House, for all the night
>   I heard the Wind of Truth; —
> I followed where it seemed to lead
>   Through all my youth.
>
> But when I sought the House of Dreams
>   To creep within and die,
> The Wind of Truth had levelled it,
>   And passed it by.
>
>   (*MH*, 3)

The language, capturing a child's voice in the opening stanzas and assuming a more mature tone in the closing, gives the poem a sense of covering all the years of growth. And the stark simplicity of the lines provides an almost incantory quality.

When the volume appeared it did not receive much critical attention. Not many people could have seen it, for it was published in an edition of only one thousand and many copies were unsold. Reedy, of course, gave it a good notice, but added, "My only objection to the *Sonnets to Duse* is that they are too intense an idealization; that is to say, to one who has lived somewhat close to the world of the stage and its people."[37] With unexpected assertiveness Teasdale sent a copy to the English poet and critic Arthur Symons, who had written an essay on Duse. He wrote an encouraging review for the London *Saturday Review,* judicious in its praise:

In this little American book there is poetry, a voice singing to itself and to a great woman, a woman's homage to Eleonora Duse. The sonnets to Madame Duse are hardly the best part of the book, for they speak and the lyrics sing; but they speak with a reverence which is filled with both tenderness and just admiration. . . . There are little songs for children, or about them, as lovely as these, and with a quaint humor of their own. The book is a small, delightful thing, which one is not tempted to say much about, but to welcome.[38]

Teasdale herself soon outgrew this early work, calling it, "so pitifully a typical 'first book'—so many of the things already sound school-girlish."[39] Modern readers will not quarrel with her criticism, but these few poems are valuable for they show how much hard work and effort she was to apply in the following years to improve her work—never satisfied, always struggling to find the word, the rhythm, the sound that would convey more intensely the emotions she felt. Certain achievement, however, had been made—Teasdale had made the commitment to a career as a poet, she had developed the discipline to work at the craft of poetry, she had taken the first steps toward making her poems available to the world. The ensuing years would test her commitment, sharpen her skills, expose her to a broader literary world.

Chapter Three
The World Caught Music

With the publication of *Sonnets to Duse* Teasdale had the first confirmation of her position as a professional poet. If its significance was primarily symbolic, it was nonetheless valuable in affirming to herself and to the world her determination to perfect her art. At the same time, however, she was beset by an internal struggle that sapped her energy and reduced her to a condition of "infantile helplessness."[1] While, on the one hand, she deliberately worked at exploring new depths in her work and widening her literary community, on the other hand, she experienced frequent lapses into serious physical and emotional illness. The four years that elapsed before the publication of her next volume, however, saw marked strides toward maturity as a poet and as a woman.

The Search for Health

Bouts of ill health had been a factor in Teasdale's life since early childhood, the legacy perhaps of her overprotective childhood during which every sniffle was treated as a serious respiratory disorder. These illnesses had frequently interrupted her association with the Potters and had caused her considerable difficulty during her trip to Europe and the Holy Land. But in late 1906 the physical element seems to have been only a part of a more overwhelming general malaise. Recovery from the physical symptoms had always been slow, but now she experienced periods of lassitude and inability to cope with the ordinary details of daily life. In the winter of 1907–8, following the publication of *Sonnets,* she suffered from an attack of such intensity that her parents sent her to San Antonio, thinking that the warmth of the South might alleviate her suffering.

Attacks of disorders such as Teasdale experienced were not uncommon in this period. According to one scholar they were due to the late Victorian demand for inordinate sexual and social propriety that seemed to inhibit every expression of normal emotion and made intense experience seem a lost possibility.[2] Even though religious scruples had been losing their hold, moral principles continued in force, laying an even greater burden on the individual to control behavior by force of will alone. And although the Protestant religion was becoming less significant in people's lives, its pattern of introspection continued, often leading to an inexplicable sense of anxiety. As Jackson Lears has phrased it, "Plagued by doubt but still driven by a Protestant conscience, introspective late Victorians felt compelled to seek relief from decision-making and responsibility."[3] The common escape route was through nervous prostration. In *American Nervousness* (1880) a New York neurologist, George Miller Beard,[4] had coined the term *neurasthenia* to cover what today would be recognized as a wide variety of neurotic symptoms all of which produced a paralysis of the will. The apparent increase of the illness after the Civil War was attributed variously to the noise and pace of modern civilization or to overwork in the struggle for existence, and although some felt that it was merely a disease of "society ladies who were either too coddled or too dissipated to shoulder their duties as wives and mothers," it struck such well-known leaders as William James, Charles Eliot Norton, and Henry Adams.[5]

With both suicide and insanity apparently on the increase, the seriousness of the ailment could not be ignored. An array of possible cures was proposed. Beard had recognized "repression of emotion" as a factor and one physician, Dr. Robert Edes, blaming social conventions, suggested that patients be permitted to scream when they wanted to "instead of restraining . . . feelings for propriety's sake."[6] But even he, as well as most mental hygienists, called instead for mental and moral control. One major approach was to view psychic energy as if it were a quality in limited supply, and to insist on withdrawal from all activities to conserve the limited resources. Such an approach could be as disastrous as the illness itself, as Charlotte Perkins Gilman so graphically displayed in her short story "The Yellow Wallpaper."[7] There the heroine is confined to a room by her husband, a physician, without any activity to relieve the monotony until she imagines other women crawling through the maze of flowers in the wallpaper. At the end of the tale the woman is completely mad.

An opposite approach is suggested by Annie Payson Call in *Power through Repose,* a book that Teasdale read. Call claimed that a cure might be found by getting in touch with one's unconscious and thus tapping new sources of psychic energies. By calling for a loos-

ening of the conventions, these therapies suggested a shift in emphasis from arbitrary standards to the needs of the growing
personality.

The medical treatment that Teasdale received for most of her life,
however, seems to have been akin to the approach of those who
supported the view that the illness was caused by limited psychic
energy. The long periods of enforced rest, originally to protect her
from physical illness, seem to have become retreats from emotional
conflicts. A serious bout during the winter and spring of 1906–7,
Drake suggests, might be due to "tension in her relationship with
Will Parrish" who "tended to be autocratic in her dealings with
Sara."[8] He describes her conflict as in part due to the struggle
between the puritanical restrictions imposed largely by her mother
and Teasdale's own sensuous nature. An entry from the notebook
she kept during her trip suggests her difficulty in separating herself
from her mother's emotional control. Writing about a sermon she
heard on board ship, she wrote that "you think that being really
good is the only thing worth trying."[9] The phrasing here, of this
need to be "good," creates the image of a child obeying its parents.
The strictures of Puritanism reinforced by Victorian conventions
that the mother advocated conflicted with the passionate, romantic
nature of the young woman, whose life thus far had been one of
continual emotional deprivation.

The problem was reinforced for Teasdale, as for many others
brought up as she was, by the pattern of thinking that viewed all
situations only in terms of polar opposites. It was a pattern of
thinking that pervaded her attitudes all her life. If she accepted her
ambitions as a writer, she would therefore lose her femininity, a
fear that informs her words in a letter written a few years later. "I
know I'm not like most of the women who write, for they love to
argue and I don't, and they are never afraid of people and I always
am. . . ."[10] At this point, her attitude toward marriage was equally
split. If she married she would be wholly a wife and mother; if not,
she would be the old maid she described in the poem:

> Her body was a thing grown thin,
> Hungry for love that never came;
> Her soul was frozen in the dark
> Unwarmed forever by love's flame.
> (MH, 6)

"The divided self" found strictures against everything she was and wanted—desire for a career checked by social restraints, aesthetic interests curbed by moral scruples, emotional depths restrained by rules of propriety, the wish to experiment and rebel controlled by the need to be obedient and to conform. With long hours of solitude enforced throughout her life and only her thoughts to occupy her, Teasdale must have frequently been tortured by the apparently insoluble contradictions of her life, and the careful scrutiny of her own inner life during those periods of introspection must have caused unbearable anxiety. That she was able to transmute these tensions into poetry is a testament to her courage; that she was frequently paralyzed by them was an unavoidable counterpart.

When the trip to Texas failed to produce any improvement, Teasdale was sent, in March 1908, to a sanitarium, Cromwell Hall, in Cromwell, Connecticut. The regime there was strict, all activity forbidden. The twenty minutes a day that had first been allowed for writing was soon banned, and even the writing or receiving of letters, except to and from her parents, was prohibited. When her recovery failed to occur speedily enough, she was moved from the main building to a cottage, seven feet square, where she had only her nurse and "some friendly spiders" for company. A fellow patient, Harriet Curtis, with whom Teasdale was somewhat friendly, described her treatment:

I must try to keep myself on one even line and not be disturbed by unhappy or very happy occurrences. He [the doctor] wants me to live for a while just an animal life, not being very interested in anything and I am "on silence" which is a particular penance now that I am among such congenial people. I thought the extreme loneliness would do me more harm than good, but he thinks otherwise.[11]

The suggestion that there was "an intensely female environment" has been discounted by Drake, who pointed out that the doctors were men and that there were men as well as women patients. The schoolgirl "crushes" to which Curtis refers can also be explained by the accepted pattern of women's behavior at the time.

Teasdale's account reveals her own ironic response; both accepting the treatment and giving vent to her irritation:

The prevailing philosophy is: "Ask yourself what you want, and then know for a certainty that is exactly the thing you should not have." Hence, if

you like cold baths, you have hot ones, and if you like to be alone, you
are told to be with people and if you hate meat, you *must* eat it. [12]

Another aspect of the treatment at Cromwell Hall is captured in a
letter Teasdale wrote to Amy Lowell some years later during another
stay: "I am taking a 'rest-cure' and it leaves me so much time to
think that I've pulled my own soul and every body else's soul to
bits—and am sick of the whole business." [13]

Teasdale remained at the sanitarium until July, after which she
traveled with a nurse for a month along the coast of Massachusetts,
not returning home until August. However punitive the regime,
it was not unappealing to her, for Cromwell Hall became the haven
to which she retreated whenever the difficulties in her life seemed
to overwhelm her.

Teasdale's first tentative steps toward emotional independence
came with her friendship with Marion Cummings Stanley, an intense, brilliant woman eight years her senior. Like Teasdale, she
was sensitive to the aesthetic ideal of beauty, shared her intellectual
interests, wrote poetry, and suffered from frail health. But Cummings valued her independence and chose to expend her energy in
reckless abandon. Married, and a philosophy instructor at the University of Arizona, she undertook ambitious projects, concerned
herself with the larger social issues of the day and seems to have
accepted more easily her right to her own career. The friendship
had begun when Cummings, who had read Teasdale's poetry in
periodicals, had written to Teasdale after she discovered a student
in her class was a personal friend. Their enthusiastic correspondence
led to an invitation to Teasdale to spend the winter of 1908 in
Tucson where the hot, dry weather might restore her health. Although her parents were fearful—she was twenty-four years old,
but had never traveled alone before—they agreed to the arrangement, provided a family maid accompanied her. Teasdale spent two
and a half months in a rented house a few yards away from Cummings. The maturity toward which she was struggling did not come
swiftly nor easily. Upon her return from Tucson, she suffered a
severe relapse and she was once again sent, from May to July 1909,
to Cromwell Hall for the rest cure.

The total adoration of her new friend was an indication of deep
involvement that was fruitful to both her emotional and her intellectual development. For the first time she had someone with whom

to discuss intimate problems. Cummings, who had to struggle for
most of her life, fought vigorously against the rest-cure approach
to Teasdale's problems, which she felt produced negative results,
and urged the younger woman to involve herself more fully in life
and in work. In suggesting some of the mind-cure approaches popular at the time, Cummings was laying the groundwork for an
investigation of the psychological causes of Teasdale's ill health. It
was probably due to Cummings that Teasdale read the book by
Annie Payson Call. Perhaps most important was her insistence that
Teasdale herself had the capacity to cure herself. The notion had a
great effect and became the subject for one of the poems published
many years later, the conclusion of which is:

> Only yourself can heal you,
> Only yourself can lead you,
> The road is heavy going
> And ends where no man knows;
> Take love when love is given,
> But never think to find it
> A sure escape from sorrow
> Or a complete repose.
>   (*MH*, 80)

Another poem that grew out of the association with Marion Cummings indicates that Cummings was urging Teasdale to continue
with her career. Teasdale speaks of a lover who "bound strong sandals
on my feet" and sent her out into the world, creating a conflict,
which the poet expresses:

> Oh, take the sandals off my feet
> You know not what you do;
> For all my world is in your arms,
> My sun and stars are you.
>   (*CP*, 21)

The tremendous growth that the relationship produced for her
poetry can be seen more clearly in the sonnet "Primavera Mia," for
in this poem Teasdale is able to merge the key poetic images that
dominated her poetry but had until then expressed conflicting lines
of thought and feeling. The full sonnet reads as follows:

As kings, seeing their lives about to pass,
Take off the heavy ermine and the crown,
So had the trees that autumn-time laid down
Their golden garments on the dying grass,
When I, who watched the seasons in the glass
Of my own thoughts, saw all the autumn's brown
Leap into life and wear a sunny gown
Of leafage fresh as happy April has.
Great spring came singing upward from the south;
For in my heart, far carried on the wind,
Your words like winged seeds took root and grew,
And all the world caught music from your mouth,
I saw the light as one who had been blind,
And knew my sun and song and spring were you.

                                        (*CP*, 33)

The first four lines use the image of medieval royalty that had
so dominated her early verse and thinking, and the description of
the trees in autumn shedding their leaves has the ponderous, funereal
rhythms that accentuate the weightiness of the act. The second four
lines reverse the seasons and the rhythmic pattern as well, moving
from the carefully end-stopped lines of the ideal sonnet form to a
freer pattern in which every line flows into the next, and the lighter
triplet rhythm mirrors the freedom expressed in the words of the
poet who now chooses to see spring in her mind despite the evidence
of the outside world. In the last six lines the greater truth of the
poet's inner sense of reality is proclaimed. Her former reliance on
the outer world represents a blindness that has been overcome.
Through the inspiration of her love she finds the combination of
light, of music, and of the creativity of spring within herself.

In many ways the poem becomes a kind of declaration of independence, of the poet's right to express her own vision of reality
even though it may conflict with the reality that the outside world
accepts. She may defy the evidence of the natural world and say she
feels spring even when the autumn leaves fall. Further, the conflict
between sound and silence that had appeared in many of the poems
in *Sonnets* is resolved in favor of sound, as the lover's words have a
creative, not a destructive, role to play, becoming the fertile image
of growth within the poet that produces her songs. And by linking
an image of light to her song and to her creativity she expresses her
right to be a poet.

These poems inspired by the friendship attest to the intellectual stimulation the association with Cummings also provided. They were both interested in many of the same authors—Gabriel D'Annunzio, Elizabeth Barrett Browning, Christina Rossetti, Théophile Gautier—and together read G. J. R. Hauptmann, Hermann Suderman, Dante, and Shakespeare. A main focus of their interest was their concern with famous women of the past. Both wrote poems about Helen of Troy and Sappho and both had a romantic idealization of beauty and love.

The friendship continued with many letters filled with romantic effusions and in the following years two visits by Cummings to the Teasdale summer home in Charlevoix, but the intensity lessened around 1910, after which the two women seem to have drifted apart. Cummings later divorced her husband and moved to New York to pursue her idealized schemes for achieving world peace. She married a professor at Columbia University and was living in the city during the time that Teasdale had made it her permanent residence, but they rarely met. Cummings's influence, however, remained a part of Teasdale's inner life, and poems she wrote many years later attest to the long-range significance of the association.

The Search for Love

The months spent in Tucson had a profound effect on Teasdale's maturation both as a woman and as a poet, but another influence would prove to be almost as important. In February 1908 she had written to a young poet, John Myers O'Hara, requesting a copy of his translations of Sappho selections, some of which she had read in magazines. From this initial request grew a correspondence and a friendship that continued for many years. Although it was begun as primarily a literary discussion—comments about their favorite authors and critiques, usually laudatory, on each other's poems—it soon contained an undertone of romantic interest. Their discussions concerned Ibsen, Matthew Arnold, and Swinburne, among others, but O'Hara seemed to use these discussions as stepping-stones to a more intimate relationship, possibly regarding the love-poems she sent to him as a covert invitation. He used their common interest in Hellenistic tradition to suggest a more unrestrained existence that Teasdale countered by insisting that, as she said in a letter to Cummings, "if I am a Pagan, I am a Puritanized one—

or else, the other way around, a Paganized Puritan."[14] Teasdale felt that he regarded her poems as declarations of love to him and he countered by urging more explicit expression. Nevertheless, O'-Hara's overtures were not totally unacceptable and aroused emotions in the young woman that may have surprised and frightened her. While a love affair by mail seems a tame sort of thing, it was the closest Teasdale at that time had ever come to a relationship with a man, and the passions it inspired in her conflicted with the conventions that had governed her life till then.

The correspondence between the two is thoroughly reviewed by Drake in his biography. His conclusion that Teasdale's puritan spirit was frightened by the sexual innuendoes in O'Hara's letters is probably merited; it certainly provided the basis for much of her discussion of the relationship in her letters to Cummings. But her reluctance to respond to his advances could also be due partly to her practical sense that this self-pitying, despairing young man was not a suitable husband for her, the only way, of course, that she could imagine their relationship.

In addition to her friendships with Cummings and O'Hara, Teasdale also developed some literary acquaintances in St. Louis, among them Zoë Akins and Orrick Johns. Akins, a friend from her school days at Hosmer Hall, was an aspiring poet who later became a Pulitzer Prize–winning playwright in New York City and well known during the first quarter of the century for her open rebellion against the social conventions. Johns, the son of the editor of the *St. Louis Post Dispatch,* worked as literary and drama critic for Reedy and was himself a poet. In his memoirs Johns talks of the Teasdale he remembers, as having "very little existence outside her poems. She was solitary, frail, and a devourer of books, modest about her own lyrics, yet confident and assured, when her stanzas satisfied her. Her delight was contagious—it was childlike, extraordinary. . . ."[15] During this period Teasdale, along with her Potter friend Will Parrish, helped Akins assemble her first book of poems. The friendships continued intermittently when all three were living in New York.

Helen of Troy

Despite the difficulties and interruptions, Teasdale continued to write. And she began the practice she was going to continue throughout her life of systematically submitting her poems to periodicals for publication. It is important to notice the kinds of periodicals she selected—*Scribners, Century, Harpers*—for they were not those that were most accessible to women writers. There were, then as now, many magazines that were edited for a female audience and included a fair number of works by women. The fiction and poems they published tended to be viewed as lesser efforts, and were judged by standards less stringent than those of the more prestigious male-oriented periodicals. The market for such publications was quite large and the number of practicing women poets was a notable phenomenon of the age. Although the topics they treated tended to be domestic and their attitude sentimental, they offered women poets an audience, as well as the opportunity to experiment with various forms of expression.

This was not a market that Teasdale was aiming for. Rather she chose to submit her poems to the most prestigious periodicals then being published in America. Cheryl Walker has noted that by the end of the nineteenth century many women like Teasdale had raised their sights as artists and were seeking acceptance from a heretofore male-dominated area.[16] Teasdale's efforts were not wholly revolutionary, but they did place her in the forefront of women poets. In these efforts she was undoubtedly aided by Reedy, whom Teasdale had called her "literary god-father," and he was a valuable guide during the early stages of her career. By 1909, when she was ready to publish a second volume of verse, Reedy urged her to seek a more reputable company than Poet Lore. But getting the volume *Helen of Troy* published was not an easily achieved task. No longer willing to bear the expenses herself, as she had done with her first volume, Teasdale sent the poems to publisher after publisher only to be rejected. The courage to persevere reminds us that however insecure Teasdale might have been in her personal relations, she had faith in her own poetic talent and the courage to make sure it was presented to the world. Finally, in December 1910 Putnam's accepted it.

Helen of Troy—Dramatic Monologues

Helen of Troy and Other Poems was assembled with even more care than the earlier volume. During the summer of 1910, when Cummings had visited Teasdale at Charlevoix, the two women had devoted much of their time to the preparation of the volume. The time and energy that Teasdale lavished on arranging the poems indicates the importance she gave to this aspect of her work, using it as a way of underscoring the values she wished to have noticed. Like *Sonnets to Duse, Helen of Troy* was primarily organized to accentuate her use of certain poetic forms, but the addition of a section called "Love Songs" accentuates a new concern with theme. In each of the later volumes this skill in organization was perfected, greatly increasing our appreciation of her work.

The most obvious difference between this volume and the earlier one is the inclusion of the long monologues, experiments with this form having begun even before the publication of *Sonnets to Duse.* Teasdale's use of the monologue differs significantly from the practice of Robert Browning, its best-known practitioner, and unless the variations are noted, her achievement is apt to be underrated. [17] Browning's concern with the dramatic monologue was to create a speaker whose values and behavior were distinctly at odds with those of the poet, thus permitting an ironic tension between the two, while at the same time the dramatic situation of the poem provides the opportunity to reveal the eccentricity of the character. In a different use of the form, that of Tennyson, for example, the persona of the poem becomes the epitome of a particular emotion or passion; it is a lyrical rather than a dramatic creation. Individuality of character is less important than the range and variety of passions displayed, and the separation between speaker and poet exists as a way of objectifying those emotions, rather than providing ironic effect.

Teasdale's monologues combine some elements of both the dramatic and the lyric form and are derived, probably, from Swinburne and the monologues in the numerous verse plays she read and reread, particularly those by D'Annunzio, Richard Hovey, Maeterlinck, and Stephen Phillips. Like Browning, she was interested in creating a personality for her speaker; but, as in Tennyson, the character's speech was an extension of feelings that the poet has perceived within him- or herself. All three approaches are, however, alike in that they create a distance between the world of the poet and that of the poem. As Carol T. Christ has explained it:

. . . the poet's dramatic presentation of material suggests an attempt to present it as an event not dependent on the personality of the poet or generated by his experience. The form at once emphasizes the subjective,

historical, and relative nature of truth while it strives to escape that
relativity and historicity by separating the poem from the experience of
the poet. . . . It at once emphasizes the relativity and contingency of
truth while it strives to transcend that relativity by making the poem an
object independent of the personality of the poet. [18]

The form was particularly attractive to Teasdale also because it
was at once a formal pattern with certain conventions that guaranteed
serious consideration by a critical community that demanded such
treatment, and at the same time gave the illusion of natural speech.
Unlike Tennyson, who accepted the traditional view of his character's world, and following the practice of Swinburne, among others, Teasdale revised the historical or legendary situation to suit her
own purpose. That purpose, above all, was to retell the story from
a woman's point of view.

Love was the dominant theme in the group, but each of the six
poems presents a different aspect of the theme—Helen, whose physical attractiveness has made her a victim of men's desire contrasts
with Beatrice, who as Dante's muse was admired and loved only at
a distance, therefore denied fulfillment. Sappho, whose passion was
transmuted to song and then to maternal affection, is placed next
to Marianna Alcoforando, who, despite her nun's vows, has known
one moment of love. The nun's moment of passion then contrasts
with Guenevere, whose life as a revered queen was destroyed by one
moment's giving in to passion, which in turn contrasts with Erinna,
Sappho's friend, who died from the lack of a lover's response. For
all these women the experience of loving has been a source of pain
and sorrow. Each one has been victimized by it in one way or another.
While the responses that Teasdale created were not uniform—Helen
becomes vengeful, Beatrice regards her desire as shameful although
not evil, Sappho finds peace through being a mother, the Portuguese
nun is absolved by the vision of the Virgin smiling at her, and
Erinna finds the dream of love's return compensation for death—
yet all end on a positive note: the experience was worth the pain
and sorrow. The six monologues all reveal the sufferings of women
in love with such force that it is difficult to believe that such was
not the poet's intent. For someone like Sara Teasdale, such a position
suggests the deep underlying resentment of the inescapable hardship
of a woman's life. And the fact that death figures in all but one of
them suggests that the two ideas were inextricably joined in the

poet's mind. At the same time, what is remarkable about these women is that they are all people who value life and the experience of living fully—value it even more than they honor the conventions of their world. Speaking through them, Teasdale could express ideas that were to become prominent in the flapper age.

Teasdale also used the collection in order to offer certain other contrasts. There are two royal figures—Helen and Guenevere; two poets—Sappho and Erinna; and two cloistered figures—Beatrice and Marion Alcorforando. Both Helen and Guenevere have lost their power, but while Helen, who lost her power through no fault of her own, vows to reassert herself, Guenevere, who took the step that caused her downfall, regrets her loss but nevertheless feels it was worth it. Sappho and Erinna present different positions toward their art—Sappho, who feels that her new love for her child is totally encompassing and more valuable than her earlier loves, gives up poetry for motherhood; Erinna, dying, considers poetry less important than the love she sought but failed to get, preferring to have people remember her as the perfect lover rather than as a great poet. Of the two cloistered figures, Marion Alcorforando was a nun who dared to break her vows for a brief moment of love while Beatrice has lived the celibate life within her father's home but regrets her lack. It is as if Teasdale was trying out alternative views about love/power; love/art; spiritual love/physical love. And in each case it is love in and of the world that is preferred, even though it might bring pain.

The character of Helen of Troy was a familiar one to readers of the nineteenth century, and Teasdale was particularly fond of Poe's poem "To Helen." Helen's character is best known today through its use by H. D. (Hilda Doolittle), Teasdale's contemporary. Written at a much later time, H. D.'s *Helen in Egypt* (1961) explores through a mixture of poetry and prose an intermediate way for women dominated neither by intellect nor emotion; her Helen is, however, like Teasdale's, an assertive woman whose relationships with men are never happy.

Teasdale drafted her poem during a three-hour railroad trip after a visit to Bessie Brey, a friend from her days with the Potters for whom she had romantic feelings and to whom she wrote the poem "Faults." She later remarked that she never enjoyed writing any poem so much as "Helen" and given its image of female revenge for masculine mistreatment, it is easy to see why its author might feel a vicarious sense of satisfaction.

Teasdale's Helen makes a choice unusual for literary women then: she chooses power. The Helen of Troy presented here bears only a remote connection to the mythic figure whose beauty made her a helpless pawn in the struggles of men. Although this Helen is seen at the moment of the burning of Troy, bemoaning her fate and begging for death, yet the vitality of the natural world—"the sound of singing winds, the strong clear scent that breathes from off the sea"—rekindles her love of life and causes her to disdain the "still wan fields Elysian." With her new commitment to life comes a new attitude. If her beauty has been the cause of her downfall in the past because men had so desired to possess her, she would now use it as a weapon against them. Her beauty will give her the power to subjugate them: "Men's lives shall waste with longing after me." She will become the epitome of all they long for but can never obtain. And Menelaus, who comes to slay her, will drop his sword when he sees her: "He shall not have the power to stain with blood / That whiteness—for the thirsty sword shall fall / And he shall cry and catch me in his arms." The last lines proclaim her triumph: "I shall go back to Sparta on his breast / I shall live on to conquer Greece again."

In contrast, the monologue "Guenevere" presents a royal figure who has dared to find one moment of love, but who, enduring the censure of the community, can only respond with confusion and bewilderment. Numerous versions of the story exist, and Teasdale was certainly familiar with the ones by Tennyson, Swinburne, William Morris, and Richard Hovey. And of these, the poem undoubtedly owes much of its inspiration to Hovey's verse-play *The Marriage of Guenevere*, although Morris's poem "The Defense of Guenevere" was also influential. Teasdale had read Hovey's play twice around 1905 and four or five times in the following years, according to her reading notebook. The portrait Hovey presents of the queen is a tomboyish figure who was "the personification of the new woman"[19] resenting social strictures that require her to be quiet, demure; "Eating her heart out at embroidery frames / Among old dames that chatter of a world / Where women are put up as merchandise. . . ." His Guenevere goes willingly to meet Launcelot in the garden. When she is discovered with her lover, she fears the punishment that Arthur will impose only to learn that he dismisses all charges against the pair. His seeming magnanimity, Guenevere realizes, is the cruelest punishment of all.

This monologue was the first of the group that Teasdale wrote, and it appeared in the April 1907 issue of the *Potters Wheel* dedicated to Hovey. The poem was published in Reedy's *Mirror* and widely reprinted in newspapers and magazines throughout the country to great critical acclaim. Its appearance probably did more to foster Teasdale's budding reputation than did *Sonnets to Duse*. Like Hovey's character, Teasdale's queen is a high-spirited woman, aware that her beauty and position in society justify her existence:

> I was a queen, the daughter of a king,
> The crown was never heavy on my head
> It was my right, and was a part of me.
> The women thought me proud, the men were kind,
> And bowed down gallantly to kiss my hand
> And watched me as I passed them kindly by. . . .
>
> (*CP*, 17)

It is not clear from Teasdale's poem, as with Hovey's, that the meeting with Launcelot had been prearranged. Her Guenevere only says:

> I walked alone among a thousand flowers,
> That drooped their heads and drowsed beneath the dew,
> And all my thoughts were quieted to sleep.
> Behind me, on the walk, I heard a step—
> I did not know my heart could tell his tread,
> I did not know I loved him till that hour.
> The garden reeled a little, I was weak,
> And in my breast I felt a wild, sick pain.
> Quickly he came behind me, caught my arms,
> That ached beneath his touch; and then I swayed,
> My head fell backward and I saw his face.
>
> (*CP*, 18)

Teasdale's ambiguity is undoubtedly deliberate, for it focuses attention on the response of the society that condemns the errant queen regardless of the degree of her responsibility. Before that fateful night Guenevere had been regarded as "a flower amid a toiling world, / Where people smiled to see one happy thing." She finds that now, "the warders at the gates, the kitchen-maids, / The very beggars would stand off from me. . . . / I am branded for a single fault." The tone that Teasdale attributes to Guenevere is one of hurt disbelief that people's opinion could change so radically: "The world would run from me and yet I am / No different from the queen they used to love."

Like Morris's Guenevere, Teasdale's queen attempts to justify herself. Morris's version follows the original by Malory closely, portraying Launcelot as Guenevere's champion on two different occasions. Morris, however, offers a suggestion that Teasdale picked up on—that her beauty protects her from association with evil: ". . . will you dare / When you have looked a little on my brow, / To say this thing is vile. . . ."

Both Morris and Hovey focus on Guenevere's response to her transgression: Teasdale focuses on society. For her the puzzle lies in its condemnation. Rather than being a cautionary tale against marital infidelity or an exposure of the weakness of women in the face of temptation as were her models, Teasdale has turned the story into a condemnation of her culture. For Guenevere the night of love has had a value that overrides other considerations, ". . . he who loved me best / Made me a woman for a night and day."

The two cloistered figures, Beatrice and Marion Alcoforando, also contrast attitudes toward love, yet both affirm a belief in its value. The monologue spoken by Beatrice, Dante's muse, presents the woman at the moment of her death, lamenting the fact that life had passed her by. Teasdale's interest in her may have been inspired by one of the reading projects Teasdale and Cummings undertook during their time together in Tucson. Teasdale's comments on the *Divine Comedy* in letters to O'Hara do not suggest any profound involvement with the masterpiece and it provides an insight into the character of her mind that she would be more interested in the artist's muse than in the philosophical poem.

As Beatrice looks back at her sheltered world, she realizes how much she has lost by her failure to live "a little closer to the ways of men." It is her regret that gives her the courage to speak to her companion Ornella, urging her not to repeat the same mistake. As death closes in, Beatrice fears her advice has been overheard, as if in having spoken such words, she had committed an evil act. The last lines suggest an ascent into Heaven, the reward for her blameless life:

> The room is filled with lights—with waving lights—
> Who are the men and women 'round the bed?
> What have I said, Ornella? Have they heard?
> There was no evil hidden in my life,
> And yet, o never, never let them know—
>
> Am I not floating in a mist of light?
> Oh, lift me up and I shall reach the sun.
>
> (*CP*, 13)

Either Teasdale did not wish us to consider the advice a sin, or she wanted the reader to believe that the words have not been heard. The lines raise once again the seemingly unrelenting fear that Teasdale had that words in and of themselves could be evil and destructive, an issue that registered itself in the conflict between song and silence that marked many poems in *Sonnets* and had momentarily been resolved in "Primavera Mia." By her ambiguity here Teasdale managed to speak out her complaint yet avoid censure.

The nun, Marianne Alcoforando, contrasts with Beatrice both in the fact that she is a cloistered nun who has taken vows of celibacy and in the fact that she dared to break them. The story comes from a volume published in England as *The Letters from a Portuguese Nun to a Cavalier,* translated from the French by Edgar Prestage. Although purporting to be the work of a religious woman who had been seduced and abandoned by a French soldier, it was in fact a hoax written by a Frenchman, G. J. Lavergne de Guillerague, in 1669. More recently, three Portuguese women have used the work as a reference point for their own feminist study, *res portugaises*.[20] Teasdale's portrait ignores the love affair itself, concentrating on the woman's reflections about her actions.

The nun is presented in old age thinking back over her life. In her musings she regards her moment of passion as like

> A cruel sun,
> That on some rain-drenched morning, when the leaves
> Are bowed beneath their clinging weight of drops,
> Tears through the mist and burns with fervent heat
> The tender grasses and the meadow flowers.
>
> (*CP*, 15)

Overcome with "love's sorrow and love's bitterness'—but not apparently bothered by the fact that she has broken her vow of chastity—

she prays before the statue of the Virgin one night and finds that the statue smiled at her. The message that Teasdale has her narrator discover is "that Love is worth its pain / And that my heart was richer for his sake, / Since lack of love is bitterest of all." Despite the differences, then, between these two women, the message is the same—seek love.

In the monologue by the nun there is a long section of praise for motherhood, a theme that is picked up again in the poem about Sappho, assuming prominence here as a way of life that surpasses her role as poet. The Sappho poem and the one spoken by Erinna, Sappho's friend, deal primarily with the contrasting goals of love and art.

The Sappho monologue is particularly important because, for Teasdale, she served as the archetypal woman artist. During the nineteenth century she was elevated to supreme stature by critics who praised her few surviving lines and by the reverence in which ancient Greek and Roman writers held her. She was a particularly important figure for American women poets. As E. S. Watts has pointed out, "Like Sappho, the American women considered themselves self-conscious artists, struggling with their environment and their art."[21] Among the American poets who had written of Sappho, she names Marie Gowen Brooks and Mary E. Hewitt. Men were intrigued as well, among them Swinburne, and Teasdale's friendship with John O'Hara had begun in response to his book on Sappho.

The particular nature of Sappho's sexuality, which had been discussed by Daudet and Baudelaire, was known by Teasdale at least by 1909 when Zoë Akins discussed Sappho and her "girlfriends" at a party that Teasdale attended. But it was the image of Sappho as a woman who combined passion and the role of the artist that Teasdale emphasized here. Teasdale was concerned with her more as an artist who transmuted her passion into poetry. Poems based on Sappho's life and legend appear in Teasdale's writings as early as her days with the Potters; two Sappho poems in *Sonnets to Duse* praised her ability as a singer. In one the poet envies her for having lived at an earlier time, "before the joy of life was half outworn," and in the second she expresses the hope that some of Sappho's lost poems may yet be recovered. In the two other poems to Sappho in this new volume there is an interesting change. Instead of wishing for the discovery of Sappho's lost works, Teasdale now talks of hearing them being sung, "Beyond the dim Hesperides, / The wind would blow such songs as these——." The suggestion is that Teasdale as a poet is re-creating the Sapphic verses as she hears them sung by the wind. The notion reiterates the mystical values of melody, now carried by the wind, to overcome distance and time. In contrast, the poem "To Cleis," addressed to Sappho's daughter, questions the child's response to her mother's passionate nature and songs, but because the child was not a writer, because there is no melody, her thoughts are lost:

> Cleis speaks no word to me,
> For the land where she has gone
> Lies as still at dusk and dawn
> As a windless, tideless sea.
>   (*CP, 35*)

It is through poetry, heard in the wind and in the sea, that death can be conquered.

The Sappho monologue in this volume grew out of the association of Teasdale with Cummings. During their winter together in Tucson both women wrote poems about Sappho that concentrated on the problems of the woman artist. In Teasdale's poem Sappho looks back at her earlier self—the self that ran passionately on the shore merging with the "hungry beach" and yearning for the sensations of sea and sand against her body.

> Am I that Sappho who would run at dusk
> Along the surges creeping up the shore
> When tides came in to ease the hungry beach,
> And running, running, till the night was black,
> Would fall forespent upon the chilly sand
> And quiver with the winds from off the sea?
>   (*CP, 92*)

Now, as a mother, she sees her life devoted to her daughter. But this new role carries for Teasdale an extraordinarily high price—the loss of her ability to sing. Motherhood brings peace but it also brings "a quiet at the heart of love." The lullabies she sings to the infant are lost, for she now sings "for one who falls asleep to hear."

Erinna's monologue is spoken to Sappho, who has come to visit her dying friend. She too has been a poet, but unlike Sappho, who has the ability to "set your sorrow to a song, and ease your hurt with singing," Erinna believes her "songs are less than sea-sand that the wind / Drives stinging over me and bears away." Sappho's "words will live forever" but for Erinna love was more valuable than her art. The man she loved, though, ignored her, and at the moment of her death she has only a dream of his kiss to sustain her.

For both of these women the love of men has been painful and the role of poet has not provided adequate compensation. While it might seem that Teasdale here is suggesting the notion that art is less valued than love, it is worth noting that she has in fact written poems in order to express that idea—in effect, she has made her point and its opposite both at the same time.

As a group, the monologues suffer from a lack of individuality in the voices; they all sound as if they were spoken by the same person. There is also a failure to create any tension that would make the moment a memorable one. The monologues were valuable to Teasdale, however, for they permitted her to investigate a number of different attitudes that women might have about love, a number of different kinds of situations that women might face, and they gave her the opportunity to express opinions that she might have felt were unacceptable if presented in her own voice. She could describe women who had known love and those who had not; women who had suffered in silence and those who had suffered but chose to fight back; she could compare maternal love with other forms. However diverse her topics, Teasdale could only imagine that love would cost women some measure of grief or deprivation; yet the tone of the monologues is not pessimistic or self-pitying. Each of the women has the strength to say what she is feeling, whether anger or bitterness or regret. And most of them speak forcefully for the values of living life to the fullest extent despite its attendant sorrows.

It is this ability to discuss subjects and attitudes that might otherwise be taboo that was of greatest value for Teasdale's development as a poet. If the question of "song versus silence" had been the crucial issue in creating so many of the *Sonnets to Duse* poems, the main concern had been whether it was right to voice complaint or to suffer in silence. In these dramatic monologues the focus had moved beyond that limited scope. Behind the mask of the persona of the individual monologues Teasdale could not only express women's reactions to the constraints their societies had imposed upon them, but also question the value of a life so constrained and assert

its worth. Like Duse, Teasdale could become the character in a play
and through that medium give voice to her most intimate feelings.
And through the magic of melody she could overcome the limitations of time and distance.

Helen of Troy—The Lyrics

The rest of the poems in this volume are primarily valuable as
attempts to find a form and voice that would best convey her ideas.
Teasdale was not primarily a theorist about her poetry, but an article
she wrote before the publication of *Helen of Troy* provides some
insight into her standards. In it she defended the practice of publishing poems in magazines, suggesting that while a poet should
write to satisfy himself, public opinion should not be ruled out.
She urged the poet to be a "sincere and dedicated artist":

Poetry is a concise and beautiful way of telling the truth. . . . If a writer
asks himself frankly and exactly what he feels about a certain object,
provided he has felt real emotion in regard to it, and provided that the
subject is worth the emotion, his answer to the question, if it is simple,
direct, and musical, will be a poem. [22]

The key terms, "real emotion," and "simple, direct, and musical,"
outline the goals that Teasdale herself was trying to achieve. But
she also added that the poet needs to read thoroughly the poetry of
the ages, indicating her respect for literary forms. However, she
emphasized the individual voice:

Every human being has something to say of himself which could not be
said by another. Never in all the ages past nor in those to come will the
same combination of emotions possess a human being as those which possess
him. [23]

The short poems in *Helen of Troy* are attempts to achieve the
standards enunciated in the article, but the variety of form and level
of skill suggest that it was easier to announce the standards than
to achieve them, for they contain numerous contradictions. The
reading public could be annoyed by the concentration on tradition
that critics might be looking for, while the critics would be con-
descending if it were absent. "Simple, direct" speech often wars
with "musical" expression, while the focus on the unique experience

poses a threat to the universality that communication demands. In her efforts Teasdale covered a wide range of material, not yet sure of what her individual voice might be nor where her individual talent might best find expression.

The use of a number of verse forms suggests that, as in *Sonnets to Duse,* this was still a primary concern. Within the book there are three-line, four-line, six-line, and nine-line stanzas; there are poems in which all the lines are the same length and those with alternating six- and eight-beat lines; there are others that end in brief three- or four-beat lines, and a few that use the sweeping Sapphic pattern of seventeen syllables to a line. Rhyme schemes vary from couplets to alternate rhymed lines to complex patterns using very few rhymes over many lines. Diction, too, was varied as Teasdale tried out various kinds of voices.

Given this wide variety, it is difficult to pinpoint any particular approach or attitude and say that this is the real, essential Teasdale except through hindsight. At this point in her career she was still groping toward her way, balancing public standards against her own, struggling to find acceptable ways to express her inner feelings. What can be done is to pay close attention to those poems that were particularly successful.

One of the most beautiful and one that captures the musicality she sought is "I Would Live in Your Love," written in 1910. It uses the long line and triplet rhythm of what was considered the English equivalent of the ancient Greek lyric associated with Sappho.

I would live in your love as the sea-grasses live in the sea,
Borne up by each wave as it passes, drawn down by each wave that
   recedes;
I would empty my soul of the dreams that have gathered in me,
I would beat with your heart as it beats, I would follow your soul as it
   leads.

                                      (*MH*, 3)

The sweeping rhythm of the lines captures the motion of the waves against the shore; the liquid vowel sounds accentuate the soothing but insistent quality of their action; the almost monotonous quality echoes the unchanging nature of the ocean. If its message of total immersion of the woman in the life of her lover seems unacceptable to modern women, it is mitigated somewhat by the fact that the

lover here is equated with the emotion of love itself so that the
poet's yearning is not only a call for a particular person, but also
the very human desire to be overwhelmed by the emotion itself.

Teasdale used medieval imagery in a number of poems, including
the verse drama included in the first edition but later removed,
replete with dreamy ladies and venturesome knights, but she found
her most successful use of it in a brief ballad in which she creates
two voices: a young man who asks where he can live without being
bothered by love and a pilgrim who answers:

> There is a place where Love is not,
>   But never a ship leaves land
> Can carry you so quickly there
>   As the sharp sword in your hand.
>   (*MH*, 4–5)

The sense of the medieval ballad is carefully maintained by the
use of certain traditional features such as the dialogue form, the use
of archaic gestures such as asking the pilgrim to swear on the sword
of the truth of his response, and also through such medieval notions
as sailing "beyond the ocean's rim." But it is the compression of
meaning that gives it such intense force. Rather than saying that a
loveless state can be achieved only in death, Teasdale merely has
the pilgrim refer to the sword as the speediest way to escape from
love. Although the time it takes a reader to understand may be only
a few seconds, even that pause permits the emotional and intellectual
impacts to coalesce to produce a minor shock.

Couched in an archaic form, the inevitability of pain and suffering
as a concomitant of desire is the poem's message. Disguised by the
archaic form, it might almost escape our attention but reveals a
level of maturity on Teasdale's part that had been frequently missed
through attention to her more girlish lyrics. This same awareness
also infuses "Vox Corporis."

> The beast to the beast is calling,
>   And the mind bends down to wait;
> Like the stealthy lord of the jungle,
>   The man calls to his mate.
>
> The beast to the beast is calling,
>   They rush through the twilight sweet—

> But the mind is a wary hunter;
> He will not let them meet.

(*MH*, 4)

This apparently simple two-stanza poem revolves around the metaphor of animals in the jungle but the reader is soon aware that the
search is within the human body. The search is not just by men,
for the beasts call to each other and rush to each other. But con-
summation is denied: "But the mind is a wary hunter; / He will
not let them meet." The use of the metaphor here is particularly
striking, for Teasdale handles it with great fluidity, moving back
and forth between the symbol and its equivalent, not so much as
to confuse the reader but sufficiently to make a statement without
being simplistic. We are aware of the split between mind and body
in the second line, where "the mind bends down to wait," but the
significance does not become clear until the last line, where reason
is described as a "wary hunter" who "will not let them meet." The
image becomes more chilling when we realize that Teasdale has
posed the human condition as a battle within each individual between hunter and hunted, locked in perpetual struggle—the body
searching for its natural fulfillment, constantly preyed upon by the
mind as the force to prevent uncontrolled bestiality. The mind here
is given the role of protecting society, guarding the social conventions, while the body is seen as the natural force toward procreation.
The split between mind and body is a long-standing tradition particularly prominent in Puritan theology, but Teasdale's use of it
here suggests levels of awareness not usually attributed to her.

Many of the poems in this book reflect the taste of the reading
public of the day, which was quite different from current standards.
Particularly popular were poems by women in which the speaker's
voice was young, even girlish, and in which the sentiments reflected
the submissive, demure, dainty prettiness of the Victorian standard
for the feminine. The image had been sharpened somewhat by the
new woman who was bolder and more independent, but the old
values did not die easily. Teasdale's success in pleasing this more
traditional audience was remarkable, and poems were praised that
would not receive a second glance today. Poems like "The Shrine"
talk of keeping "my altar fair" so that a Lord will come to her heart,
while another, "The Rose and the Bee," begins with "If I were a
bee and you were a rose, / Would you let me in when the grey wind

blows?" The critic for the *Literary Digest* particularly praised the line in "The Song Maker"—"I made a hundred little songs"—and called "The Christmas Carol," a description of the adoration of Christ at his birth with the image of the child falling asleep during the hymns, "the best poem in *Helen*."[24]

For modern readers the value of these poems lies in ways Teasdale used the conventions to circumvent restrictions on what was proper for a woman to write. One frequent device was to empower the things of nature with the gift of speech. A number of these appear in "A Maiden" (*CP*, 23–24), in which the poet first says that if she were a rose she would climb into her lover's window; then if she were a bird, "All day I'd sing my love for him / Till he should harken me." In the concluding two stanzas, however, she points out that "Since I am a maiden / I go with downcast eyes, / And he will never hear the songs / That he has turned to sighs." In the conclusion she adds, "My love will never know / That I could kiss him with a mouth / More red than roses blow." The poem is wonderful in its duplicity. On the one hand, it honors the restrictions on what a proper woman would do and say; on the other hand, it manages to say exactly what the poet wants. The poet, through the verse, manages to announce that she wants to get into her lover's room by visualizing herself as a climbing rose; she is able to say she loves him by imagining herself as a bird; and she also indicates her physical desires by saying her lover will never know the pleasure of her kisses. Teasdale uses the wind as a substitute spokesperson, sometimes the flowers, but her more frequent image is of the bird, which as Cheryl Walker has pointed out,[25] was a dominant figure for women's poetry in the nineteenth century.

Another device that insured her popularity with traditionally oriented women readers was to make use of the voice of the child-woman as in "The Kiss," noteworthy because it not only meets a popular image of girlish spontaneity, but also manages to convey an ironic view. "The Kiss" has the transparent surface that Teasdale had spent so many hours perfecting, its simple language and easy flow providing a sense of total effortlessness that mocks the difficult technique it requires. In it the speaker tells about being kissed by her lover, as she had hoped, but finds herself heartbroken because "his kiss was not so wonderful / As all the dreams I had." There appears to be no problem understanding such a verse, yet a closer look reveals a depth of unsuspected meaning. Part of the power of the poem comes from the sense of distance between the poet and the speaker in the poem, much the same as would be achieved by a dramatic monologue. The voice is extremely childish in its naïveté, melodramatic in the hyperbole of her equating her condition with that of a "stricken bird that cannot reach the south." It is the voice of a girl who has lived so long in her romantic dreams she is doomed to be disappointed by reality. It is a poem that makes us smile with the same kind of tender compassion we might feel toward a disappointed child. At the same time it confirms our own superiority; *we* know what reality is like and would never make the same mistake. And what is that mistake? Partly, it is believing all romantic tales of love and marriage that were the staple of the Victorian age. But partly, too, it is accepting the role society had imposed on women, forcing them to stand by and wait for a lover to come to them, with only dreams to fill the void, impossible dreams that only grow more grandiose the longer the wait. Teasdale's tone is lightly ironic, but it is worth noticing that the young woman speaking is very close to the kind of woman who just a few years earlier wrote the worshipful sonnets to the adulterous actress Eleonora Duse.

Of all the poems in this volume, "Union Square" attracted the most attention and brought her the greatest notoriety. It was one of the group of six poems written about New York City, which Teasdale had visited early in 1911, and these poems were printed together though not labeled as a separate section. The other five deal with such diverse sections of the city as Coney Island, Gramercy Park, Central Park, the Metropolitan Museum of Art, and the tower of the Metropolitan Life Insurance Building, reflecting her excited explorations of the city. Though arranged in no particular order, each poem seems to describe lovers walking together, the birth of love, its growth, its joys, and its ending. "Union Square" exists in a number of versions. In the notebooks that survive there is a version dated 30 March 1911, but its title, "New Version, Union Square," indicates that an earlier form had been written. Unlike the final version, the 1911 version talks not of love, but of death, and the focus is on the "picture shows, where the crowds went in to half forget, / the grave where each man goes." This version was an attempt to revise the one finally printed, to make it more socially acceptable. The published version contrasts the condition of the woman narrator who must keep silent about her love with the condition of the prostitutes on Fourteenth Street who openly solicit for their trade. The poet's envy of their freedom is caught in the final lines, "But oh, the girls who ask for love / In the lights of Union Square" (*MH*, 6). The idea that a proper young lady would even notice, much less comment, on the existence of prostitutes was something of a shock to the literary establishment and the reading public so that they hardly noticed the underlying naïveté of the poet who assumed that what the "girls with thirsty eyes" were seeking was synonymous with love. The hesitant rebel that Teasdale had become is captured in many ways in this poem—in her anger at her forced silence, in her daring to mention the unmentionable. It was a poem that Teasdale at first did not feel she should publish, but on the advice of friends decided to include. It made her volume seem much more adventurous than the total contents actually present. And it was this feature of the book that was most frequently commented on in the reviews.

The four years that elapsed between the publication of *Sonnets to Duse* and the appearance of *Helen of Troy* were marked by significant steps forward in terms of technique, widening subject matter, wider audience, wider literary community, and growing independence from her family. But the period was marred by frequent breakdowns in mental and physical health. Each step forward had taken its toll, but she had continued to move forward.

Chapter Four
Sandaled with Wind and with Flame

The period between the publication of *Helen of Troy* and *Rivers to the Sea* showed Teasdale's growth and maturity as a woman and increasing development as a poet. In those years she discovered the literary communities of New York and Chicago and traveled again to Europe. She broadened her social world, and her growing national reputation as a poet both increased her self-confidence and sharpened her critical faculties. Periods of illness and depression still marred her life as she faced conflicts between her puritan heritage and the new hedonism, between desire for a career as a poet and her wish for the conventional life in marriage. But she was healthier during these years than she would ever be again. At the end of 1915 she would have both a new, best-selling book of poems and a husband, providing the illusion that she could balance both her artistic ambitions and her feminine role. The poetry she produced during this period shows a growing ability to transmute her personal experiences into art. She no longer fretted in her verse about her right to be a poet, and she integrated the themes of love and beauty into a new relationship that formed the basis of her art.

The event that brought her out of the limited world of St. Louis was the invitation she received to join the Poetry Society of America. This organization, which had been founded in October 1910, admitted poets by invitation only and was intended to lend an air of both importance and respectability to the profession. The aims of the organization were discussed in an article in the *New York Sun* in March 1911.[1] Pointing out that in an age of science and commercialism, poets, as well as artists of all sorts, are apt to be ignored, the writer added, "The land rings with the truest poetry, though its voice might be smothered in the anvil chorus of our amazing activities." The goals of the association were to "secure for the art of poetry fuller public recognition as one of the more important forces in a higher civilization . . . . kindle a fuller and more intelligent appreciation of poetry . . . [and] stimulate the production of high class poetry."

Teasdale's name had been proposed by Madison Cawein, a popular poet from Louisville, Kentucky, who was a friend of a St. Louis admirer of Teasdale's. Teasdale was eager to attend the annual dinner of the society in New York City in December 1910, but persuading her parents to let her go (although she was now twenty-six years old) took much effort, requiring the approval of her doctor and permitted only after her parents were assured that the Parrish sisters, old friends from St. Louis now living in New York, would look out for her. Although she did not actually get to the banquet, she was able to attend the monthly meeting in February 1911, where she was thrust into a major literary community. Some of the names of the people she met are still familiar to us, but many have faded from the public mind as the kinds of poetry they were writing were not intrinsically valuable enough to survive the changes in literary fashion.

One of the most important persons she met was Jessie B. Rittenhouse, the dynamic secretary of the society, herself a poet, journalist, and lecturer on poetic trends. She immediately befriended Teasdale and the two women began a friendship that was to last for the rest of Teasdale's life. Through Rittenhouse, Teasdale met other members of the literary community in New York and eventually in other areas as well. Rittenhouse herself was valuable not simply as a friend but also as a role model, a woman who seems to have accepted the idea of a literary career without the fear that she would thereby lose her femininity. Other women Teasdale met also seemed able to combine the two goals. They may have had the value of lessening Teasdale's anxiety on this point.

Among the members of the Poetry Society and of the New York literary scene with whom she became friendly over the next few years were Louis and Jean Untermeyer, Joyce and Aline Kilmer, Padraic and Molly Colum, Edward Markham, Margaret Wilkinson, Margaret Widdemer, John Reed, Edna St. Vincent Millay, Stephen and William Benét, Elinor Wylie, John Hall Wheelock, William Stanley Brathwaite, Witter Brynner. She established a friendship later mainly through correspondence with Amy Lowell in Boston, and occasionally visited Harriet Monroe and the group of writers who lived in Chicago.

The influence of this community was significant, for it provided more stringent intellectual standards than she might have received in St. Louis. The attitudes of the Poetry Society, though, were essentially conservative, following Rittenhouse's view that poetry should reflect change but avoid the revolutionary; and their discussions of Teasdale's work reflected standards that seem quaint today. For example, at a reading at a Poetry Society meeting, her splendid lyric "I Shall Not Care" was the subject of an argument over whether it was, as one member described it, "charming," or as Joyce Kilmer called it, "tragic," or even as a third said, "It has a humorous effect on me because the writer is evidently playing with serious emotions. He's trying to be tragic, and he knows he's trying to be tragic."[2] Modern readers would recognize that it is precisely the juxtaposition of these emotions that produces the poem's force, but the standards of the day called for a singleness of mood and purpose, and critics attempted to categorize poems as one form or another.

This poem, reminiscent of Rossetti's "When I Am Dead, My Dearest," is one of Teasdale's most popular, not only in her own day but for generations after. It achieves such an extraordinary harmony so liquid that its sound patterns threaten to engulf its content.

> When I am dead and over me bright April
>   Shakes out her rain-drenched hair,
> Tho' you should lean above me broken-hearted,
>   I shall not care.
>
> I shall have peace, as leafy trees are peaceful
>   When rain bends down the bough,
> And I shall be more silent and cold-hearted
>   Than you are now.
>
>   *(MH, 5–6)*

The poem also presents a pattern that Teasdale used to great advantage—the announcement of a position or a description of a scene in the opening stanza, resolved with an unexpected or ironic twist in the closing. The brief half-line ending of each stanza, the standard practice in the Sapphic tradition, lends a sense of weightiness and finality to each part of the poem. Her adeptness with this particular form was so great that, in fact, it threatened to make the extended reading of many of her poems together seem monotonous and formulaic, often obscuring the real virtues of any particular one, a point stressed by a contemporary critic.[3]

New Locations

One major value of these years was quite simply the new landscapes with which she came in contact, expanding the subject matter of her poetry. Neither the pleasant suburban streets where she lived, nor the factories and warehouses of the waterfront at St. Louis had appeared to her as fit subjects for her verse. In fact, there is only one poem about St. Louis, written some years later, and that gives a traveler's view of the city. But New York, with its dazzling lights, its tall buildings, the hustle and bustle of its streets, even its subways, buses, and trolleys, was exhilarating, romantic, even exotic. The wish to capture the emotion it produced was the impetus to a significant number of poems written during her first trip, a few of which were added to *Helen of Troy*. The romance with New York was not a short affair but one that intensified during these four years, producing numerous poems. The views from the towers of the city gave her a sense of a godlike view of human life; the crowded streets gave a sense of human vitality, the populousness of the world, the varied types of people, the beggars, the shabby poor, and, as we have seen, the prostitutes—the range of human experience. Even the waterfront with its hints of travel to exotic far-off lands appealed in a way that the river front in St. Louis never did. The parks were seen as encapsulated pastorals, providing trysting places for young lovers. Above all, the atmosphere seemed to reek of hedonism. Her amazement at the city was captured in a sonnet that found its lights more impressive than those of Babylon and Rome, as if the city had "found a god and filched from him / A fire that neither wind nor rain can dim. / One that even rivals the stars." In a poem written during the last years of her life Teasdale described New York as a "Princess, lithe and swaying lightly / Above the housewife cities of the earth," suggesting that the image of medieval heroines had found a wider significance for her.

In 1912 Teasdale added still further to her poetic landscape through a trip she and Rittenhouse took together to Europe, a period she called "the most memorable season of my life." Although she had

been to Europe previously with her mother in 1905, this trip seems
to have been especially pleasant. The happy mood inspired a great
many poems, most of which would appear in subsequent volumes.
One, however, reflecting the dangers of too much sight-seeing by
hungry Americans presents a lighthearted side that was often omitted from her collected works:

> I'm tired of all the quaintness
> And the faded fresco's faintness
> Of dusty musty sacristies
> With saints along the walls;
> I'm very sick of Giotto
> And Massaccio and Lotto,
> And of dingy Lady chapels
> With black worm-eaten stalls.
>
> (*MH*, 11)

Even more valuable than the sights of Europe in terms of expanding her poetry was the renewed acquaintance with the ocean.
The long voyages to and from Europe brought back the awareness
of the force of the sea, which she had noted on her first trip, and
now the image became one of the most potent in her work. Both
in its totality and in its separate parts, it provided images in her
poetry, treated throughout her life with subtle shifts of meaning
and implications.

The Search for Love

Romance, however, must have seemed to the young woman the
most exciting results of her new life. The courtship-by-correspon-
dence that she had been carrying on with John O'Hara, unfortunately, was dissipated at their first meeting in New York when she
discovered that, despite his frequently seductive letters, he was
unprepared for serious commitment. Her disappointment and anger
probably were responsible for the serious emotional and physical
relapse she suffered on her return to St. Louis after her first visit,
but it was also something she was able to transmute into art, producing a brief story that was eventually published in 1916 in H.
I.. Mencken's *The Smart Set*.[4] The revenge she achieves is in the
portrait of the man in the story who is obviously modeled on O'Hara.
In the story he is a constant visitor to the heroine, making regular

visits marked by propriety but a total lack of emotion. He seems to enjoy the affection that the heroine offers him, but does not appear capable either of returning it or of realizing that he has raised her expectations about possible commitment. What emerges is a figure of a man totally lacking in passion in any of its forms. The heroine, finally daring to take action on her own, invites him to her country home, but while she waits expectantly and fearfully for his arrival, she receives a telegram announcing that he is sailing for Europe instead. As a view of a woman in love, the story gives a sense of what Teasdale regarded as the fate of the woman who dares to speak up for herself in matters of love. The crushing pain of rejection she experiences, Teasdale seems to be saying, is what such a woman should expect. Such a conclusion underlines the fact that Teasdale, while moving ahead as a poet, was still bound by the conventional limitations on a woman in a romantic relationship.

The trip to Europe in 1912 with Jessie Rittenhouse provided her with a new romance, for on the return voyage she met Stafford Hatfield, an Englishman gifted in music and literature as well as science. Described as "outgoing, even mercurial,"[5] he charmed the young woman and apparently hinted at a desire for a more intimate friendship, the precise nature of which cannot be pinpointed at this late date, but did not apparently include marriage. Teasdale was obviously smitten, for she remained in New York during the few weeks of his stay there rather than returning immediately to St. Louis as she had planned. The shipboard romance did not, however, mature in the ways Teasdale had hoped, and by the time Hatfield sailed back to England, she was in a state of such frustration and despair that her friend Will Parrish had to bundle her back to her home. The serious depression that followed may have sharpened her latent thoughts of suicide. It lasted for several months, producing a group of bitter poems she labeled "The Progeny of Hatfield," the best known of which is "The Old Maid."

The most confusing of her romantic entanglements during this period was her relationship with John Hall Wheelock, a poet and editor at Scribners. The friendship began while she was still in St. Louis through a correspondence in which they praised each other's poetry. It solidified during her third trip to New York in 1913. Wheelock became a regular caller while she was there and together they explored the city. Wheelock said in an interview many years later that he did not realize that Teasdale held romantic illusions about him until it was too late to explain his true situation of attachment to another woman whom he was not then able to marry. Instead, he permitted Teasdale to hold romantic hopes about him without ever explaining his failure to return her affection or to explain his actions. Teasdale continued to believe that he was in love with her despite his failure to say so and after one evening together, according to Wheelock, she murmured, "You love me and I love you."[6] His failure to respond must have left her confused, for she continued to entertain hopes of marrying him up to the point of her engagement to another man. Wheelock was the object of her deepest affections and his presence can be felt in many of the poems she wrote during this period. Even after her marriage, Wheelock continued to be a close personal friend, an intimate to whom she confided her most pressing problems, and his concern and care for her lasted all her life. Their relationship also depended on their professional interest in poetry and they offered critical suggestions to each other throughout their careers.

The literary community that centered around the Poetry Society and many of the other writers in New York welcomed Teasdale and made this rising young poet a part of its social activities. Jean Untermeyer, one of her close friends, described her during this time:

Sara lacked that touch of bewitchment that was so much a part of Edna Millay's youthful personality. Nor did she manifest at first the force of mind and incisiveness of character that was so outstanding in Amy Lowell. She was slim and tall, with sandy hair and eyelashes, and her coloring was subdued, even to the clothes she wore. It was only after a while that one noticed the extremely delicate texture of her skin, and how the faint rose would come into her cheeks, and fine gleam into her eyes, when she felt at ease and could give way to an animation that was easy of misinterpretation. She was by nature more shy than reserved. Once she felt confidence in her company she gave of herself freely, and seemingly without second thought.[7]

The number of luncheons, dinners, theater parties, and trips to the opera to which Teasdale was invited during her New York visits was so overwhelming that she had difficulty husbanding her physical resources, for she continued to be frail and prone to respiratory infections. During one week alone she turned down twelve different invitations. Such exciting times made her return trips to St. Louis all the more depressing. In her letters from her hometown to Will

Parrish in Germany she complained vigorously, "Oh, lucky that you are, to be out of this STODGE hole of a city. . . ."[8] Her stays in St. Louis were made more difficult by the fact that both her friends Orrick Johns and Zoë Akins were in New York and also by the failing health of her parents. As Louis Untermeyer rather dramatically phrased it, "She saw herself a lonely princess growing old in a crumbling tower, a virgin Sappho chained to the rock of St. Louis."[9]

Despite the careful management of her social life, Teasdale experienced several bouts of ill health and severe depression frequently on her return home, but she did avoid the sort of illness that required hospitalization. Limitations on her social life were necessary for her career as a poet as well. She devoted much of her reading time to keeping up with the works of the new poets she was meeting or hearing about. Rittenhouse's anthology, *The Younger American Poets,* and separate volumes by Markham, Santayana, Untermeyer, Kilmer, Reed, and E. A. Robinson, as well as all of Wheelock's work, which she read over and over again, are listed in her reading notebook. And she also continued to read the classics, particularly as William Drake notes, during periods of unhappiness—Plato, Aeschylus, and Euripides from ancient Greece; Fielding, Sterne, Goldsmith from eighteenth-century England; Turgenev and Dostoyevski from Russian literature; more modern English masters like Wilde, Shaw, LeGallienne, Chesterton, Hardy, and Masefield.

Her output of poetry increased dramatically during these years, for the enlarged horizons provided much inspiration for poetry, which Teasdale did not neglect. While we know only the dates when finished poems were actually recorded in her notebook, she seems to have written them in on the date of composition, noting whenever she delayed the transcription. During the period from May 1911 to the end of that year, after her visit to New York, she produced thirty-four poems. During the second visit to New York, from January until April 1912, she wrote twenty-eight and, on the trip to Europe with Jessie Rittenhouse, nineteen additional, including the long "From the Sea," with seventeen more, plus the monologue "Sappho" during the rest of the year. Back in New York in January 1913, she found herself again writing with increased vigor, producing twenty-two poems by March. Forty additional poems were written between her return to St. Louis and the date of the first version of *Rivers to the Sea,* which she presented to Wheelock in October 1913.

The main subject of all these poems was love and it is interesting to speculate on the lovers involved. The 1913 poems are mostly inspired by her association with Wheelock, and those from late 1912 by her friendship with Hatfield. Some of the 1911 and earlier 1912 poems are based on her dreams about a relationship with O'Hara, but many of the others, especially those from early 1911, cannot be traced to any particular person. She herself said that many of New York walks described in the poems were taken with no lover at all, only with her friend Will Parrish. As such, the poems represent an intensity of emotional feeling for Will, or they may be more about Teasdale's being in love with the thought of love. In many instances, the superficiality of the emotion suggests that the experience itself had not happened.

Although the subject of the poems remains close to those of her earlier work, the contact with a wider literary community brought significant changes in her technique. Most obvious were the abandonment of archaic forms, a limitation on the number of personifications, and fewer references to the medieval fairy-tale world. She had always worked to achieve a natural flow of language—almost all of her poems had always followed the normal structure of the sentence and only in rare instances are there inversions in natural word order. Now, however, she was better able to be both musical and simple.

This ability is reflected in the revisions she made in the poem originally called "Song," later "The Hour," and finally published as the first poem in "Over the Roofs," written in February 1912. The first version of the poem, which was entered in the notebook and presumably regarded as finished, reads as follows (words in parentheses are alternate versions written in the margin):

> Oh clock set high on the sunny tower
> Ring on, ring on unendingly,
> Make all the hours a single hour
> For when the dusk begins to flower
> The man I love will come to me.
>
> (might)
> Yet do not hasten—there may be
> (lest there be)

> Some girl who loves as much as I
> With charming eyes that scarcely see
> Praying for an eternity.
> Before her moment of Good-bye.
>   (Poetry Notebook)

The only change made in the first stanza was to substitute the word *chimes* for *clock*. The improvement in harmoniousness is immediately apparent, yet the new word, although a bit quaint, is neither incongruous nor pretentious. The changes in the second stanza are far more sweeping and revelatory. Her first attempt at improvement produced the following:

>   (might)
> But wait! For someplace there may be
>   (lest there be)
> A girl who cares as much as I
> Standing beside her love while she
> Prays for a whole eternity
> Before her moment of Good-bye.
>   (Poetry Notebook)

The change of "Yet do not hasten" to "But wait!" provides a more natural, less archaic tone to the poem; the reader can almost hear the sound of the speaker's voice. The rest of the line continues to have trouble and the numerous changes indicate Teasdale's unhappiness with it. "Someplace" is too vague and its placement in the line confuses the rhythm. "There may be" is wordy, but the biblical "lest there be" conflicts with the voice of the opening words. The changes in line two do not seem to accomplish much and were made, probably, because of the decision to use the word *love* in the next line. Here the improvement is more obvious. The original "With charming eyes that scarcely see" makes little sense, while the new line at least provides an image of a woman standing beside her lover that concretizes the poem. The change in the conclusion to a present-tense verb instead of a gerund sharpens the imagery, the effect unfortunately destroyed by the melodramatic pretentiousness of "a whole eternity" and the capitalized "Good-bye," suggesting a despair that is unsupported by the incident being described.

The final version, written several days later, shows Teasdale's sharp critical sense:

> But no! Go slowly as you will,
>   I should not bid you hasten so,
> For while I wait for love to come,
> Some other girl is standing dumb,
> Fearing her love will go.
>
> (*CP,* 76)

The impetuosity of "But wait" has become the more rueful "But no" and the mournful *o* sounds are repeated in "Go slowly," whose heavy beats echo the sound of chimes, tying the second stanza to the first not only through content but also through sound patterns. The focus on the narrator of the poem rather than another person, which is accomplished by the revision of line two, provides a unifying persona, rather than the former dominance of the narrator in stanza one and a second person in stanza two. The second girl is subordinated but not eliminated, appearing in the conclusion in a more natural way of "standing dumb." The force of the poem derives from the careful contrast of the words *come* and *go* foreshadowed by the rhyme scheme, their almost gonglike quality referring the reader back to the opening. The common habit of most people to group *come* with *go* creates a tension when the word *come* is used, as we wait for its opposite. The relaxation of that suspense with the final word of the poem insures that the ending will provide a sense of completion. It is only a simple, ten-line poem, but its artlessness is the result of the hard work and sure ear of a skilled poet.

Teasdale was not a theorist about her poetry at this time, but in a letter to Professor Curtis Hidden Page, written in 1912, she indicates other ideas about poetry while providing a clue to the scholarly attitudes toward poetry at the time. Page had apparently written to her about *Helen of Troy and Other Poems,* criticizing the lighthearted tone of a triolet about Dante and Beatrice as suggesting a lack of respect for such a giant of literature. The demand for reverence was one of the Victorian standards that Teasdale had experienced as part of her childhood training but, as is apparent here, her concern for it in poetry was not merely personal; it was an expected mode of behavior from the reading public she hoped to impress. And Page's criticism, while it did not change her practice, did cause her to be more covert. Professor Page also complained about "At Night," to which Teasdale responded, "A quatrain is very often like a nut, when it ought to be a flower. This one is a nut, without a doubt—and not a very *good* nut either. That is the trouble with too much compression, it has the tendency to make your work hard."[10] She added, "cleverness is the very last thing one ought to have in poetry, isn't it?" It is important for modern readers to realize that many of the standards that have developed over the past sixty years are the exact opposite from those Teasdale had for herself.

Rivers to the Sea—First Version

In October 1913 Teasdale presented Wheelock with a sheaf of poems assembled for possible publication as a volume. Wheelock described the incident as an interview and, despite his somewhat laconic tone, suggests the nature of Teasdale's feelings for him:

[She] showed me the slowly growing collection of the poems that were to form her next book, as yet without a title. She had come to have an exaggerated regard for my critical judgment, where poetry was concerned, and consulted me constantly on what to leave in and what to take out. I gave my opinions freely, for whatever they might be worth, and she acted on them often; not always, however. The question of a title for the volume troubled her greatly. Many were proposed and discarded, until one day I suggested "Rivers to the Sea," part of the second line of the last stanza of a poem of mine, without title, on page 11 of my third book, *Lover and Liberation,* then recently published. Sara had taken a special fancy to this poem. Her approval was instant. With characteristic impetuosity, she blazoned the new title across the first page of her manuscript, striking out all the other, tentative ones. About a week later, if memory serves me, Sara came to the Scribner Book Store and handed me a package that I was not to open till I went home. Impatient, I untied it almost the moment she was safely out of the store, and found in my hands the autographed manuscript, complete up to that date, of what was to appear in 1915, after certain additions and subtractions, as one of Sara Teasdale's most important books, *Rivers to the Sea.*[11]

The collection Teasdale showed Wheelock represents a significant step forward from her work in *Helen of Troy,* yet is sufficiently different from what she was to achieve in the 1915 version as to warrant discussion as a separate entity. It marks Teasdale's emergence as a mature artist.

One significant advance was the arrangement of the poems within the book, a factor that was always a primary consideration for Teasdale. Instead of accentuating the formal elements of her work by titles she gave to sections within the manuscripts, as she had with her two previous books, she emphasized either a storylike arrangement of a group of poems or the particular image being used. Several sections in this version tell of the birth and death of love affairs, the narrative element providing a sense of flow that prevents monotony, an approach she said she copied from George Meredith's *Modern Love.*[12]

The first such "story" is entitled "First Love" and the thirteen poems include two of the four sonnets written for a project suggested by O'Hara for a joint book about New York, her relationship with him perhaps providing the reason for the title. "Broadway" is marked by the skillful handling of the opening lines where the control of the rhythm underscores the meaning. "This is the quiet hour . . . ," the rough junction of "quiet" and "hour" forcing a pause that stretches out the line beyond its metered length.

In one of her letters to Will Parrish Teasdale mentioned this poem, in which she had originally included the line "For love above us like a banner stirs." About the line she said, "meaning, of course, to bring to mind the old phrase in Solomon's 'Song of Songs' 'His banner over me was love.' But it's not just the sort of thing I wanted to say at this point, for it's too far away from a feeling of Broadway."[13] Her decision to change the line may have been confirmed when she later received the letter from Page criticizing her for irreverence.

Particularly fine were the lyrics "To One Away" and "The Kiss," which opened this section and the book. Although she was to continue to use the notion of a bird or flower carrying her message, the poet now communicates with her beloved through her own gift of words, through the poem itself. The heavy iambic beat of the lines is softened by a few carefully placed triplets. The sense of compression in the short last lines suggests the rhythm of a heartbeat. "The Kiss" is particularly beautiful in the sensuousness of tactile sensations where wind and rain become caresses transmuted into sound, yet the movement within the poem is of the caress becoming destructive "As rain puts out a star. . . ."

Another section entitled "Songs in a City" describes a love affair that takes place in the city—which, although unnamed, is undoubtedly New York. Four poems grouped together as "Over the Roofs," the only ones that actually use city imagery, tell of a woman who moves from sureness of her lover's affections to awareness of his infidelity. With a novelist's care she foreshadows the disappointment in the first poem by the narrator's awareness that her happiness is contrasted to the misery of others, and in the second by a warning she attributes to fate. The remaining poems tell of the torment of unfulfilled love that she imagines will continue even after death.

The poems grouped under the title "From over the Sea" tell the story of a trip to Europe and, although the titles of individual poems indicate places such as Gibraltar, Naples, Algiers, the locations are more evocations of romantic settings as backdrops for thoughts of a lover. Jessie Rittenhouse, in her memoirs, mentions Teasdale writing these poems and says that "with happy spontaneity she would toss off lyrics of the passing scene."[14] A closer study of Teasdale's notebooks shows, however, that practically all of the poems based on the trip were subjected to careful reworking. Landscape in these poems reflects the late Victorian practice of using settings "to evoke fleeting, lyrical, otherwise inarticulable emotions essentially independent of nature,"[15] yet demanding some specific objective reference—the "few toads in an imaginary garden" that Marianne Moore called for.

This series of poems also deals with a love affair, following an autobiographical pattern. This is not a first love but is connected with a man met on a ship and continues after they have reached land. The lover is apparently untrue, for the poet's voice changes from joy in love to, first, petulance in "Song" at her lover's fickle response to her love. She senses its futility and wonders why her ability to love is not sufficient. At the end, there is only sadness and bewilderment that the beauties of the earth are insufficient for happiness and an awareness of the value of her poetic gift as compensation for pain, ending in the affirmation of "Song" for the joy she finds in poetry.

As important as this new narrative arrangement of poems within the volume was the new prominence given to imagery, specifically, the images of the city and of the sea. Teasdale's use of the city in poetry represented something of an innovation; although the urban landscape had appeared in poems of social protest, Teasdale adapted it to traditional lyrics. The city is, of course, mainly New York, but others such as Rome, Paris, and Hamburg are mentioned. The beauties of Europe are its cities; New York is, however, the treasure. A few New York poems had been interspersed among the poems in the previous volume, *Helen of Troy*; here they are given prominence by having a separate section, although there are additional poems dealing with the city in other parts of the collection. The very absence of nature in the city is, in one instance, a plus. There she says that while nature's cycles will change the forest from spring to winter, the city streets remain the same, thus preserving memory:

> The forest has forgotten us,
> But in the city well I know
> A certain street remembers still
> Tho' spring and winter come and go.
> (Poetry Notebook)

On the other hand, the absence of the natural world makes it difficult for her to remember spring ("April"). The sounds of the city and its lights provided a kind of enchanted show that seemed to have been put on for her benefit, as special in its own way as the scenes of meadows and forests were in theirs. But Teasdale was never a descriptive poet, a poet of landscapes or cityscapes, and the particular scenes are used mainly to accentuate a mood, sometimes cheerful as in "May Day," where the bustle of Fifth Avenue matches the enthusiasms bubbling within the narrator, or uncaring as in "In a Subway Station," where the "hunted, hurrying people" ignore the pain of the couple in their midst just as the lover has ignored the poet's unvoiced sorrow. The city also offers images of sensuality, most explicitly in "Broadway" and "In a Restaurant."

Even more important than images from the city to Teasdale were images from the sea. She went so far as to entitle a section "Foam in the Sea," although the bulk of the poems have little to do with, or even make any mention of, the sea, and some of the better poems about the sea are placed elsewhere. This fact stresses only more strongly the importance that Teasdale wanted to give to this image. A few poems in *Helen* had made mention of the sea, most notable "I Would Live in Your Love," where the nurturing power of the sea provides a sustenance the poet feels the lover's affection can give her. But those poems are interspersed within the volume. Now, however, Teasdale is announcing a major new focus of her poetry.

The sea image was valuable particularly because it was capable of conveying many different, even conflicting, meanings. The separate part of the sea could also represent different meanings. The foam of the sea was equated with her joy in love, suggesting both its brilliance and its brevity ("Foam"). In another lyric the foam represents her physical self as she asks her lover to "hold me as the sea holds the foam" ("The Flight"). The tides of the ocean could represent in their ebb and flow, the give and take of life ("Peace"); or they could represent its insistent nourishing, which quenches a thirsty soul ("Tides"); or the tides themselves might be thirsty ("The River"). The image of the waves focuses more on desire, the yearning expressed in their constant and futile pounding against the seaside cliffs ("Sea Spray"). Or they could suggest both sensuousness ("Sea Longing") and the inevitable ending of desire ("The Tides"). Seen as a whole, the sea could be given human emotions such as weariness when she says, "night unveils the stars / Over the tired sea" ("The Return"); or it might be a sleeping woman wearing islands on her breast ("Songs from over the Seas"). It might be a presence from whom the poet asks for guidance and receives only silence ("Amalfi").

The sea could be the controlling force that moves her restless heart although she longs for the peace of the harbor. The sea could be an alternate lover whose kiss might taint the mouth of the beloved ("The Kiss"), or it could turn the freshness of the river to bitterness. Whatever meaning she might choose, though, the sea would always be some sort of insistent life force, as in "Hamburg," where she hears, when lovers meet, the "whole deep ocean / Beating under the foam."

Many of these varied uses of the image come together in the sonnet "Sea Longing" where the beneficent and destructive powers of the sea are joined.

> A thousand miles beyond this sun-steeped wall
>   Somewhere the waves creep cool along the sand,
> The ebbing tide forsakes the listless land
>   With the old murmur, long and musical;
> The windy waves mount up and curve and fall,
>   And round the rocks the foam blows up like snow, —
> Tho' I am inland far, I hear and know,

> For I was born the sea's eternal thrall.
> I would that I were there and over me
>   The cold insistence of the tide would roll,
> Quenching this burning thing men call the soul, —
>   Then with the ebbing I should drift and be
> Less than the smallest shell along the shoal,
>   Less than the sea-gulls calling to the sea.
>
> (*CP,* 73)

The first ten lines present a sensuous scene in which cool, singing waves caress the rocks while the foam is as white and ephemeral as blown snow. The use of the word *quench* in line eleven both repeats and turns from the pleasant quality presented. As the tides quench the soul, they are satisfying its thirst; but as they quench its burning, they also put it out, thus destroying the self, a destruction that the poet craves in order to merge with this profound natural force. The poem is interesting for its ability to combine the sensuous and the destructive, foreshadowing many poems about the sea that would become some of Teasdale's most potent verse. In its ability to juxtapose oppositions in a harmonious frame the poem represents Teasdale's highest goal for herself as a writer.

The crowning achievement of the volume was the long monologue "Sappho." Although Teasdale was well versed in all the legends and scholarship about Sappho, she revised them in order to create her own sense of the ancient poet. The particular legend involved here was the one that claimed that an overwrought, insane Sappho had committed suicide over her unrequited love for the ferryman Phaon. To Rittenhouse Teasdale wrote that her Sappho would be "self-possessed," not "the passionately hysterical Sappho" that was most commonly depicted.[16] It may be that Teasdale was fighting off her own suicidal tendencies and, in fact, the manner of the suicide that Teasdale chose—quietly slipping away at night while everyone sleeps—is uncannily accurate for certain types of personalities, as Drake has pointed out.[17]

The poem questions very basic assumptions about the meaning of life, beauty, and the value of love. And her revision of the legend was also a revision of her own concept of the poet. Writing to Untermeyer, she said, "My conception of Sappho is undergoing a considerable change. I am beginning to see her not so much as a woman love-torn (or lovelorn) but as a real priestess of passion."[18]

The whole meaning of life for Teasdale's Sappho is love. As the poem traces the last moments of Sappho's life, pausing to take a last look at the walls, bed, and floor of her room with their memories of "ecstasy and sleep . . . when a gale of joy lifted my soul and made me half a god," she is aware that beauty will continue without her, for other "girls shall come in whom love has made aware of all their swaying beauty," a beauty that will be captured in their song. Beauty continues, too, in the birds in spring "over long blue meadows of the sea, and south-wind playing on the reeds of rain" (*CP*, 87).

As the narrator walks through the streets, she notices the garlands of flowers on the doorposts and prays for the people asleep that "every lover will be given love." She goes slowly so that her footsteps do not waken the people who might question where she is going. It is only at this point that Teasdale makes the terseness of the concluding lines underscore the businesslike metaphor with which she describes her main function in life, "the gods have given life— I gave them song; / The debt is paid and now I turn to go."

Through the figure of Sappho, Teasdale has attempted to state her new sense of the role of love in the life of a poet. It is the ability to love, the experience in and of itself, that has sharpened her perception of the beauty around her. Describing one of Sappho's loves, she has the poet say,

> . . . we used to walk
> Here on the cliff beneath the oleanders
> In the long limpid twilight of the spring,
> Looking toward Lemnos, where the amber sky
> Was pierced with the faint arrow of the star.
>   (*CP*, 88)

The exquisite beauty of the scene exists because of love. For a poet, however, that beauty must find expression. Talking of the other members of the community, she says, "How should they know the wind of a new beauty / Sweeping my soul has winnowed it with song?" Love reveals beauty; beauty inspires song. But at a cost— each love will remove a layer of her soul, as the chaff is winnowed from the wheat. Pain then is the inevitable concomitant of the process. But the poet is chosen by the gods to experience the pain of love, to perceive beauty, and to transmute it into song; therefore, the poet has no choice but to fulfill her destiny.

With this poem Teasdale had rationalized both her ambition to be a poet and the suffering she was experiencing as a woman in love. No wonder she was so excited that she mailed off a draft of the poem to both Rittenhouse and Untermeyer even before she had completely revised it. The ideas she expressed here were to become the central themes of the final version of *Rivers to the Sea*.

Chapter Five
Songs . . .
Free as the Wind

As exciting and productive as the New York experiences had been to Teasdale, they were accompanied by two other events that were as, or more, significant for her future development as a woman and as a poet. These events, curiously intertwined, were her connection with the poetry group centered in Chicago and her subsequent marriage to Ernst Filsinger.

Chicago and the "New Poetry"

During one of her visits to New York Teasdale had been introduced to Harriet Monroe, famous today for the periodical she was in the process of founding, *Poetry, a Magazine of Verse*. Teasdale's initial impression of the woman was hardly favorable; she described her as "not a lovable person on first acquaintance" in a letter to Louis Untermeyer[1] and was unimpressed by the new venture, adding in a letter to Marion Cummings that "I hate the fostering of an art so well able to take care of itself as poetry. . . ."[2] What these rather hasty judgments fail to take into consideration are the radical changes in poetry that were about to sweep the poetic community and the place of Monroe's magazine in fostering the new movement. What was then called the "new poetry" incorporated many elements that were being tentatively tested by many practicing poets and grew out of a number of Victorian and Romantic sources although it claimed to be anti-Romantic, anti-Victorian, "clear, hard and unillusioned." The philosophy behind the movement was best enunciated by Ezra Pound and its best-known works came from the group associated with him—T. E. Hulme, Richard Aldington, H. D. (Hilda Doolittle), and T. S. Eliot, although other practitioners, such as Amy Lowell, were already involved in similar experiments. While the tenets themselves were far stricter than actual practice, they did define a mode of vision, one that concentrated on a scientific approach in which the human consciousness is seen like a machine in which forces are exerted and produce inevitable results. A significant factor for Pound was the effect of simultaneity—that is, that the stimulus and the resulting mental processes that make up the effects should appear in the poem as if they had occurred at the same time. As Pound said,

The arts, literature, poesy, are a science, just as chemistry is a science. . . . The arts give us a great percentage of the lasting and unassailable data regarding the nature of man. . . . No science save the arts will give us the requisite data for learning in what ways men differ.[3]

The poet conveys experience as if it had just occurred to him, as though the vision was a passive inflowing of something out there like the image forming inside a camera—but, of course, it would include the affective responses as well as the external stimuli.

The principles as Pound, Aldington, and H. D. expressed them were:

1. Direct treatment of the "thing," whether subjective or objective.

2. To use absolutely no word that does not contribute to the presentation.

3. As regarding rhythm: to compose in the sequence of the musical phrase, not in the sequence of the metronome.[4]

The dilemma presented by these principles was the peculiar one of deciding what the poet's role might be. If the poem is simply a recording of observation conceived as a completely objective, non-purposive process and the observation is to be recorded without interpretation, then all that is left to the poet is to put it into verse. Free verse would thus require only technicians, like a carpenter, as Amy Lowell said in her preface,[5] or poetry becomes then "not an expression of personality but an escape from personality" as Hyatt H. Waggoner has put it.[6] The poet is like a Pavlovian dog and the theory is a denial of responsibility for the thing happening or seen.

The results of this new approach to poetry are well known and the masterpieces it produced—Eliot's *The Waste Land,* Pound's *Cantos* and H. D.'s *Helen in Egypt*—have become the classics of our day and need no discussion here. What does need to be considered, though, is the often-forgotten fact that when this poetry first ap-

peared it was only one of a number of experiments that poets were
undertaking and that arguments in favor of revising traditional
poetry instead of abandoning it continued to be more important for
many poets, including Teasdale. Harriet Monroe had founded *Poetry*
in order to publish not just Pound's brand but all kinds of writings
and artwork. A glance at any of the issues of the magazine during
the 1910s will show a wide variety of experimentation as well as a
significant amount of traditional verse, with the "new poetry" actually taking up only a small percentage of the total. Among the
experiments that appeared in the periodical were the bardic chants
of Vachel Lindsay and the sweeping lines of Carl Sandburg.

A major reason many poets resisted the new approach could be
explained simply in terms of timing—they, like Teasdale, had come
to maturity as artists by developing their craft according to the
strictures of the traditional verse and for them the conventions were
not a liability. As Teasdale was to say later—

There seems to be a feeling that if more of us could free our poetry of
lines having approximately the same number of syllables, and stanzas each
having the same number of lines, we should be happier and better poets.
But is it not evident to the editor that fairly regular rhythm, modified
by variations within itself, and regular recurrence of rhymes are joy and
freedom, not bondage, to those poets who choose them of their own free
will and who use them with ease?[7]

One very obvious reason Teasdale did not readily adopt the new
poetry was quite simply that she had been writing the old way since
her teenage years at least, over fifteen years ago. Immense amounts
of effort had gone into perfecting her craft in the light of the older
standards and she was about to reap the rewards from all that effort.
It would seem a pity to disregard all that skill in order to adopt
what might be only a passing fad. In addition, psychological factors
may be equally important in explaining Teasdale's reluctance to
venture into this new area. As in other situations, her interest in
rebelling was counterbalanced by her respect for established values.
Writing poetry was for her revolutionary enough; writing poetry in
a revolutionary style would set her dangerously outside the conventional barriers. Teasdale would always want to keep at least one foot
in the established community as she ventured into the unknown.
Moreover, conventions provided distance as well as a known technique for universalizing personal emotions.

Significant as those explanations might be, they are less important than the fact that the new poetry specifically ignored the one value that Teasdale prized above all others—the melodic quality that made her call her verses "songs." Her responses to the music of words noted in early childhood had been nourished by tonal qualities of nineteenth-century writers like Tennyson and Swinburne, for whom it was the epitome of poetic art. Teasdale's concern with it bordered on mystical—the sounds of birds, of the wind, of the sea, were lyric messages that she heard and translated in her poems like the music of the spheres that Milton spoke of as the organizing principle of the universe. The harmonious music of poetry existed not to enhance the content, but for itself alone. Only a few years later she was to write that she preferred traditional forms to the new poetry "because melody seems to me to be so magical a thing. Indeed we must admit its magic because many lyrics having little else besides melody have become priceless treasures of our race." Using Shakespeare's "Under the Greenwood Tree" as an example, she went on to say, "There is not a single, striking phrase in the song, neither is there an image nor even a deep emotion. Yet by virtue of the magic of melody alone, it succeeds in giving us deep and everlasting delight."[8] Modern readers, unaccustomed to giving such weight to melody, need to reconsider their standards when judging poetry like Teasdale's and acknowledge the basic appeal of melody.

It would be a mistake, however, not to recognize the number of ways Teasdale incorporated the attitudes of the new poetry into her own work. For one thing, she began dealing with subject matter that had not been considered "poetical"; the urban landscape in particular had already become a source of poetic inspiration in *Helen of Troy and Other Poems.* The poems in that volume had for the most part focused on the parks, those bits of pastoral enclosed in the city, or centered on the traditionally poetic, such as the museum as a repository of lost ancient cultures but at least one poem, "Union Square," had dealt with a theme more common to literary naturalism and had attempted to catch the urban feeling, emphasizing the poet as the recorder of the immediate experience, an experience that for increasing numbers of Americans was in the city.

In addition, Teasdale's poetic diction after 1911 reflected the simpler, more straightforward diction of the new poetry: the hyphenated adjectives ("flower-sweet" face) and personifications of abstract qualities ("Silence," "Pain") were in the process of being eliminated; a greater sense of compression marked her lines. It also marked the end of her looking back to medieval times, and a move toward looser rhythms. She may have been more influenced by certain aspects of the new poetry than she herself realized.

However much Harriet Monroe was drawn by Ezra Pound into becoming publisher of his brand of new poetry, she continued to be interested in including traditional verse in her magazine. Teasdale's relationship with Monroe and other poets centered in Chicago developed during a trip she made there in June 1913, on her way from her parents' home in St. Louis to their summer house in Charlevoix, Michigan. Her reactions to Monroe were substantially changed during that trip; now she found her to be "a woman so sensitive and loving that she is crying out for affection and yet is so repressed and shy that everybody thinks her old-maidish and hard and bitter."[9] They became close friends during the ensuing years and Monroe's critical acumen affected the direction of Teasdale's poetic maturity.

It was in Chicago, too, that Teasdale came in contact with a more bohemian literary community and her shock at their behavior, however amusingly she described it in her letters, may also have been instrumental in her rejection of the new directions they were taking. She wrote Jean Untermeyer, "You see SEX written over every inch of it. It is fairly screamed at you. . . . It is my sense of taste as well as my conventional bringing up that is jarred horribly by this. It seems to me to be an ugly thing—just ugly."[10]

In a curious way Teasdale's love life and subsequent marriage were closely tied to the new friends she made in Chicago. In 1914, approaching thirty, she seems to have become desperate about marriage. Although many of the women she was friendly with were spinsters, it was obvious that it was a role she could not accept for herself, at least in part for economic reasons. Unlike Rittenhouse or Monroe, she considered herself too frail to undertake a full-time job that might make her self-supporting. Nor did the enforced chastity of spinsterhood appeal to her sensuous nature and she could not, like the bohemian group she had met in Chicago, nor like her fellow writer from St. Louis, Zoë Akins, indulge her hedonistic impulses outside conventional bounds.

Candidates for marriage were presented by her friends in Chicago. Harriet Monroe provided the introduction to Vachel Lindsay, then a rising young poet whose romantic vision both encompassed the exotic worlds of Africa and Asia and glamorized the land and the ordinary peoples of America. Filled with exuberant energy, he dazzled Teasdale and for a while bombarded her almost daily with fifteen- or twenty-page letters urging her to abandon the sophistication of New York to return to her own Midwest and to join him as a singer of the American countryside. He was, unfortunately, penniless, with little hope of ever earning the kind of income Teasdale was accustomed to having at her disposal and absolutely needed, for she was totally incapable of managing a house, had no domestic training whatsoever, and required long rest cures with frequent medical attention.

The candidate who could provide for these needs was Ernst Filsinger, a St. Louis businessman, an admirer of Teasdale's poetry for years, whom she met in the spring of 1914. Introduced by Eunice Tietjens, another friend she made during her Chicago visit, he courted Teasdale in a much more cautious fashion, and only when urged by Tietjens to make his feelings more known did he pursue Teasdale with any vigor. Both biographers have presented full discussions of the courtship, and the romantic implications, particularly for Lindsay's poetry, have been treated by many others. But she clearly enjoyed the competition for her hand that developed between Lindsay and Filsinger. Like an adolescent, she must have been flattered by the attention that she had never before enjoyed. Whether she had given up her romantic interest in Wheelock, though, is less easy to decide. She made a one-week visit to New York in September 1913, to discover his feelings toward her and stayed five months, but at the end must have realized her hopes were groundless. She consulted all her friends in making her decision, and it is clear that the choice was less a question of finding a true love than an economic and social necessity. Also, she now considered having children, as the number of poems she wrote on the subject suggests. Her decision to marry Filsinger was, given that proviso, the obvious choice, but there is also reason to believe that Teasdale was trying to convince herself that she also loved the man in the romantic fashion that her reading had led her to expect. She had gained in maturity from her abortive romances with O'Hara and Hatfield, but she also must have kept some lingering notions of a mystic union of love-and-marriage.

Her marriage to Filsinger took place in December 1914, and the honeymoon, described in idyllic tones to the families, was, as Wheelock later reported, a disaster.[11] Filsinger was, according to Whee-lock, at thirty-four years old, totally inexperienced, having perhaps accepted the Victorian code of sexual behavior that modern audiences tend to forget was, in theory, as strict for gentlemen as it was for ladies. It is also possible that he had less interest in physical love than the stereotypes of masculine behavior assume to be the universal situation. The excessive adoration that Filsinger had for his wife represented an intense idealization, for he had admired her from afar for many years before their meeting and knew many of her poems by heart. There was a "most hushed portentousness when he spoke of her verse,"[12] according to Untermeyer. But such worship could also inhibit a normal love relationship, which might seem to be a kind of violation. Together they presented an image to the outside world of an enormously happy couple, and it is safe to assume that the mutual respect and affection they had for each other supplied the basis for a warm relationship, even though it may not have been the overwhelming love affair that Teasdale had dreamed about.

They settled in St. Louis, where Filsinger's shoe business was located, living in a residential hotel in order to spare Teasdale the burden of managing a household. Filsinger was extremely proud of his wife's poetic achievements, and there never seems to have been any conflict over the fact that her career would take precedence over domestic duties. Filsinger's business was, however, in a precarious state, and he not only spent long hours trying to save it, but also worked as consular representative for Costa Rica and began the arduous task of finding a new position with another firm. Their married life was further complicated by a new illness that she developed. The period of courtship had been remarkably free of ill health, but a few months after her wedding, she developed a serious bladder infection that lasted for a year and a half and necessitated two separate hospitalizations and treatments that were so painful as to be called sadistic.[13] Eventually, Filsinger took a position as foreign representative of a textile concern with an office based in New York City, and in 1916 they set up their permanent residence there although his work would, of necessity, involve a great deal of travel.

Rivers to the Sea

Perhaps in compensation for her disappointment, Teasdale turned back to her poetry, which she had seriously neglected during the

period of courtship and early months of marriage. But the main
thrust of her efforts was to prepare a new volume of poems for
publication. The original version of *Rivers to the Sea,* which she had
shown Wheelock in October 1913, underwent drastic revision before
it was submitted to Macmillan and revised yet again before it was
accepted. There were 103 poems in the final version. Fourteen in
the original version were omitted; forty new poems were added,
and of these, thirty-one (including part 3 of "Sappho") were written
in the interim period. Many of the new poems show a freedom to
investigate new forms, a sharper ear, less of the girlishness and more
of the mature woman, less need to explain her meaning and more
reliance on the poems to speak for themselves. A few of the poems
that she culled from her notebook from earlier years are among her
finest, omitted from earlier books because perhaps they may have
seemed too self-revelatory. The most significant difference was the
rearrangement within the volume to accentuate certain themes that
were obscured by the previous order.

The rearrangement of part 1 involved mainly the combining of
the separate "love stories" of the original version into one, but the
number of poems was greatly expanded by the addition of twenty-
two poems, of which twelve were composed after the Wheelock
manuscript had been completed, and the elimination of fourteen
poems from the original version. As with all of the earlier versions,
the love story traces the growth of love, the lover's joy in their
passion, a separation, and the end of that love. While many poems
retain the "girlish" tone expected of women, the new arrangement
and several of the new poems indicate significant areas of growth
as Teasdale moved toward poetic and emotional maturity.

The choice of "Spring Night" both to open this section and to
open the volume, stresses an issue that had become basic for Teasdale
as a poet and a woman—the relative values of beauty, love, and
song. The poem expressed its meaning not only through its words,
but also through the forms and rhythms that were employed.

> The park is filled with night and fog,
>   The veils are drawn about the world,
> The drowsy lights along the paths
>   Are dim and pearled.
>
> Gold and gleaming the empty streets,
>   Gold and gleaming the misty lake,

The mirrored lights like sunken swords,
  Glimmer and shake.

Oh, is it not enough to be
  Here with this beauty over me?
My throat should ache with praise, and I
  Should kneel in joy beneath the sky.
Oh, beauty are you not enough?
  Why am I crying after love
With youth, a singing voice and eyes
  To take earth's wonder with surprise?
Why have I put off my pride,
  Why am I unsatisfied, —
I for whom the pensive night
  Binds her cloudy hair with light, —
I for whom all beauty burns
  Like incense in a million urns?
Oh, beauty, are you not enough?
  Why am I crying after love?

                        (*MH*, 12)

Written in 1913 and buried in the manuscript she had shown to Wheelock, it becomes in its new placement a declaration of fresh focus for her verse, suggesting a dichotomy that will be resolved into a new synthesis at the end of the volume. In its literal meaning the poem presents a scene of exquisite beauty in two four-line stanzas, followed by sixteen lines in couplets in which the poet decries her inability to be satisfied. The divisions within the poem's structure emphasize the division the poet feels—the serene, placid tone of the first two stanzas versus the rapid, almost staccato quality of the couplets that follow. This polarity is further heightened by the careful construction of the opening section in which the second stanza almost perfectly reflects, even in its grammatical structure, the words and images of the first just as the lake mirrors the scene about it. The subject of the opening stanza, the park, is shrouded in darkness and its sleepy mysterious quality is heightened by words like "veils," "drowsy," "dim and pearled." The sentimentality that threatens to be cloying is immediately balanced by the more sharply described scene in the second stanza. Now color and light dominate in "gold, and gleaming," and the hidden qualities of the first stanza develop a more ominous tone with the image of "sunken swords."

Even the rhythms and sounds work to make the contrast more apparent—the soft *o*s and *ah*s of the first stanza are replaced by the harsher *ee*s and *a*s of the second, while the lighter iambic rhythms of the first become more ominous trochees in the second. The subject of the two stanzas also provides an important contrast, the park suggesting a pastoral world apparently peaceful but veiled, while the street lights suggest the more urban landscape in which an unknown violence is concealed.

The change in rhythm is the most obvious difference between the opening and closing portions of the poem; they differ also in that the opening is in the form of statements while the end is all questions. To the six full questions with the repeated "why" can be added two others crushed together so that the whole section is nothing but questions, suggesting the overwhelming quality of the poet's confusion. The language here has a natural quality compared to the more stylized diction of the opening, and the number of lines that are not end-stopped contrasts with the traditional measures of the opening. Not only is Teasdale suggesting here that her previous adoration of beauty is insufficient, she is also announcing a new source of imagery—the city—for her poetry. The inclusion of the city poems in *Helen of Troy* was not, she seems to be saying, an incidental increase in the range of her subject matter, but part of a different perspective she plans to bring to her work.

The issues that underlie these poems were central to Teasdale and to poets like her who were seeking ways to break out of the rigid, limited view of life with which they felt themselves saddled. The cult of beauty, the stilted "poetic diction," the use of lyric poetry only for the natural world—those were some of the standards that Teasdale is saying here she will challenge. Yet, at the same time, she proves herself to be, in the first section of the poem, superbly capable of working within that tradition. She is not saying that she will discard the tradition in order to adopt a wholly new one; rather, she is establishing her right to integrate the old within the new in order to expand poetic horizons. The balance of oppositions—traditional versus free form, love versus beauty, statement versus question—has been achieved.

The closing poem of this section provides one of the answers to these questions. "A Prayer" enunciates the poet's determination to seek love regardless of whether her love is returned. Although it is in the spirit of the Victorian poems of moral uplift, like "Invictus," it makes significant changes in direction: rather than relying on the speaker's strength of will, it is a prayer to some unnamed deity for permission or the power to experience that closest of human relationships; and instead of seeking self-control, the poet asks for total immersion in the experience. The final poems in each of the ensuing sections provide further answers to the questions posed in the opening. Within the most conservative, traditional form, then, Teasdale was suggesting a fairly radical notion—a woman's joy in loving for itself alone, not as submission to a particular man. The conflict between the adoration of beauty and the desire for love that had dominated the opening poem is resolved by the closing in the idea that the worship of beauty is a result of the ability to love and, incorporated into it, becomes the source of song.

Within the frame of these two poems of part 1 lies the story of a love that roughly follows the seasons of the year from spring to spring. The poet, in the first flush of a new romance, worries whether an earlier lover might not intrude ("The Flight"), whether having a new love does not indicate a loss of fidelity or fickleness on her part ("New Love and Old"). She worries that she will not forget her former friend ("The Look"). Love, at this point, is focused on the particular object of love. The transition provided by the next two poems establishes that the power of love itself is stronger than the ability of the individual to withstand it ("Spring"). The next fifteen poems sing of the joy of loving and being loved. They speak of the specialness of a lover's kiss, surpassing the kiss of nature ("The Kiss"), the sense of fulfillment that comes from loving and being loved ("Peace"), the sense of power and freedom she derives from love ("Joy").

But in developing the growth of this particular love affair, Teasdale is also showing how her appreciation of the beauty of the natural world deepens through experience. The vision of the sleeping swans in the park at night becomes more potent because of the slightly erotic tone with which their love endows it ("Swans"). This poem, representative of the new work that Teasdale was producing, shows her new ability to let the poem express its own meaning.

Night is over the park, and a few brave stars
Look on the lights that link it with chains of gold,

> The lake bears up their reflection in broken bars
>   That seem too heavy for tremulous water to hold.
>
> We watch the swans that sleep in a shadowy place,
>   And now and again one wakes and uplifts its head,
> How still you are—your gaze is on my face—
>   We watch the swans and never a word is said.
>
> > > > > > > > > > > (*MH*, 14)

The heavy alliteration is carefully controlled and the liquid *l* sounds and sibilant *s* suggest the mysterious quality of the scene. In another poem the sudden sight of a bluejay in a winter landscape becomes the more ecstatic because of the loving glow with which the lovers view it ("A Winter Bluejay"). The poet becomes the very items of nature that had been objects of beauty to be adored—

> I am the pool of blue
> That worships the vivid sky . . .
> I am the pool of gold
> When sunset burns and dies . . .
>
> > > > > ("Peace," *CP*, 47)

or

> I am the still rain falling,
>   . . . Oh be for me the earth.
>
> > > (*CP*, 48)

It is because of love that these scenes acquire their special intensity and permit that special perception from which beauty stems. Because of their love, even mundane scenes take on a special sheen. The rooftops and bare trees of a courtyard view in the rain become portents of spring because of love ("April"). The city streets crowded with shoppers ("May Day"), the abandoned streets in the theater district in New York glow in "liquid splendor" through their love ("Broadway"). Love can make up for past suffering, the "lonely years, / That strove to sing with voices drowned in tears" ("The Years") and for the calls of natural beauty to which she had been unable to respond ("April Song"). Love can conquer present troubles, making the two lovers, for a moment, conquerors of "sorrow, futility, defeat. . . ." And it may even prevent the future pain and ugliness of spinsterhood ("The Old Maid"). Love can even conquer distance ("At Night").

Perhaps most important, love can lend a significance to life even as Teasdale had once imagined that beauty could.

> Come, for life is a frail moth flying
> Caught in the web of the years that pass,
> And soon we two, so warm and eager,
> Will be as the gray stones in the grass.
>
> ("Come," *MH,* 27)

By joining the present to past generations ("To a Castilian Song"), love can even win out over time.

The parting and the end of the love bring to a close this group of poems, but although the events bring sadness and wilder fluctuation of themes and emotions, the values derived from having loved and been loved ultimately dominate. Love survives in the moment of parting by the refusal to show emotion ("In a Railroad Station") and continues to exist as "a timid star" in her heart ("In the Train") or as a voice in the night ("To One Away"), but her growing awareness that she is no longer loved produces a flippant response ("Song"), on the one hand, and a cry of sorrow on the other ("Deep in the Night"). Self-recriminations ("Desert Pools"), thoughts of death as revenge ("I Shall Not Care"), or lack of fulfillment ("Longing") crowd in. But compensations that she had found in having known the lover ("Pity") gradually give way to a broader range of values. Her love will be a guide to him ("After Parting"); there is value to being on the same earth with him and to feeling his love even at a distance through memory ("Enough").

The greatest value, however, comes when she is able to see in the landscape around her a way of using the pain, realizing that love has permitted her "to change the lifeless wine of grief / To living gold" ("Alchemy"). The beauty of spring, now "eager terrible" was to be found because she had known love ("February"). Spring works its magic once again as "longing lifted its weight from me" ("Morning") and gives her what will become her saving grace "I catch my breath and sing" ("May Night"). The pleasure of singing is reinforced as she observes the early evening: "Oh let me like the birds / Sing before night" ("Dusk in June"). Although she now feels free of love, she is aware that she is still her lover's

("Love Free"), and the memory of their nights together in Riverside
Park now speak to her of the eternal nature of love and the awareness
of all the lovers who have shared moments like they once knew
("Summer Night, Riverside"). Returning to the city, she remembers
a special moment where love passed them by ("In a Subway Station"),
and although a sense of apathy intrudes ("After Love"), the fact of
love outlives the particular moment of love ("Dooryard Roses"), and
on this note she is able to exclaim in the closing lyric, "Oh let me
love with all my strength / Careless if I am loved again."

This opening set of poems is, then, far more than a random
collection of verse, or even just the simple telling of a love story,
as it was in its first version. By the careful arrangement of her poems
Teasdale has accomplished several objectives: she has modified her
reverence for beauty as the force in her life, seeing it now as an
attribute of the force of love; she has expanded the focus of her
interest to include the cityscape of New York with its crowds, its
towers, its dingy streets, even its subways, as well as its magical
lights and parks; she has changed her notion of love from the finding
of a particular lover to the value of the ability to love for itself, and
she has begun to see her ability to sing—to write poetry—as the
quality that will be the most important force in giving meaning
and substance to her life.

The poems in this first section cover a variety of forms and subject
matter. Replacing the separate sections on the city and the sea, in
the early manuscript version, the poems are mingled together. Short-
rhymed stanzaic lyrics sit next to long, rhythmic, free-verse works.
Sweeping, flowing lines of Sapphic form are set against common
eight-beat, six-beat stanzas of the hymn; sea images and city sights
vie with those of the birds and starlight, trees and clouds. In "From
the Woolworth Tower" the poet sings in a melodic form of free
verse the praises of the elevator, the electric lights of the city, "a
thousand times more numerous than the stars" and in "From the
North" she even speaks of missing the subway. The different images
and forms are not separate—they flow together to form a unified
world for the poet. Where once the natural world had provided her
with a sense of refuge from society, she now finds it within the
city. The sonnet "In a Restaurant," one of those that she wrote for
the book she had planned to publish with O'Hara, vividly captures
the sense of protection in what must have seemed then the most
unlikely of places. The unnamed protagonists, presumably a young

couple, leave the dark, snowy streets and enter a glamorous world of hot lights, rich aromas, the clamor of music and laughter. The cold sterility of the outside world sets off the feverish, erotic tone of the room. The puritanical side of Teasdale is forgotten as she notes the free-flowing wine and the woman who kisses her lover in public. Yet this place is presented as a shelter, its sensual appeal a refuge from somber winter.

Of the new poems that were added, some of the most interesting are the longer ones done in free verse. One of them, "The Lighted Window," was written with Filsinger. Teasdale was still an apprentice in this form and had not discovered how to deal with the diffuseness and "prosiness" that are its pitfalls. And she was still learning to control the diction, to confine it to that of ordinary speech. But in "The India Wharf" and "Summer Night Riverside" she began to make good use of the form. "The India Wharf" describes the memory of a walk the narrator had taken with her lover and is probably modeled on the walks Teasdale had taken with Wheelock. During the walk the couple leave the avenues, "rivers of light," and enter the "narrow knotted streets" with their tense crowd of foreign people until they finally come to the river, "to water black and glossy" and a shabby building called the India Wharf, at which point they turn back. The last lines with their slight echo of Coleridge's "Kubla Khan" suggest the lost possibility:

> I always felt we could have taken ship
> And crossed the bright green seas
> To dreaming cities set on sacred streams
> And palaces
> Of ivory and scarlet.
>   (CP, 53–54)

The lushness of the closing imagery forces the reader to review the walk as a metaphor for the journey to physical passion—from broad well-lit avenues of the known, rational world to the dark, foreign, twisting streets of emotion to the ultimate immersion in sensuousness.

"Summer Night Riverside" is more explicit in its description of lovers and their passion. It tells, again as a memory, of two lovers watching the river from the park, of climbing down the riverbank to embrace under the blossoming trees. The poet/narrator, speaking a year later, wonders

> Tonight what girl
> When she goes home,
> Dreamily before her mirror shakes from her hair
> This year's blossoms, clinging in its coils?
>
> (*MH, 27*)

The poem is notable for its use of color and texture—the river wears "her lights like golden spangles / Glinting on black satin" while "the frail white stars moved slowly over the sky." The image of the lovers sheltered by "a tree that dripped with bloom" suggests the affinity of sensuality between the natural and the human world and a nurturing quality of the harmony captured in the falling rhythms of the lines. The careful placing of accented words as in the opening "the wild soft summer darkness" and in the closing "this year's blossoms," stretches out the lines and gives them added strength and significance.

Part 2 catalogs the sorrow of life. The opening poem speaks to one of humanity's deepest sorrows, the coming of death, and the poems that follow number all the disillusions that life brings. Passion, sexual desire, once thought to be a source of joy, is now seen as a source of pain. To the "pool in a peaceful place," the wind brings "the far-off terrible call of the sea" ("The Sea Wind"). The roving cloud, "child of the heartless wind," keeps hearing the pines whispering "Rest, rest" ("The Cloud"). The inhabitants of the Poor House lacking all the pleasant qualities of life, are even denied the surcease of death: "They have never lived," he said, "They can wait to die" ("The Poor House") while the invalid faces either pain or death ("Doctors"). The vulgarity of human behavior ("New Year's Dawn—Broadway"), the horror of war ("Dusk in War Time, Spring in War Time") destroy any illusion of the goodness of the human species.

Certain key themes are particularly emphasized. One is the awareness of fickleness. It is presented in a lighthearted way in "The Rose," where the woman being serenaded throws a flower she had picked when she was with another man. It assumes a deeper significance in "Dreams," where the narrator tells of having given ". . . my life to another lover, / I gave my love, and all, and all—" yet dreams of a former love affair and feels "on my breast a kiss is hot." The most difficult knowledge to face, however, is presented in "I Am Not Yours," in which the poet-narrator admits that she

has not been able to find in love that union that destroys separate
personalities. The starkness of the lines accentuates the poignancy
of the confession.

> You love me, and I find you still
>   A spirit beautiful and bright,
> Yet I am I, who long to be
>   Lost as a light is lost in light.
>
> Oh plunge me deep in love—put out
>   My senses, leave me deaf and blind,
> Swept by the tempest of your love,
>   A taper in the rushing wind.
>   (*MH*, 22)

In the closing stanza the narrator begs for passion, but the poet has
realized the limits of her own ability to love. Through the narrator,
Teasdale may also be protesting the inhibitions that Victorian morality placed on men as well as on women. Having created an
idealized figure of woman, men were expected to treat her in some
delicate fashion while what she really wants is the full force of
passion.

A theme prominent in this section is that of motherhood, an idea
that appeared in Teasdale's letters during this period. One of the
reasons she had given for wanting to be married was so that she
could have children and Filsinger had written his parents that she
would rather be a mother than anything else.[14] The evidence in the
poetry here, however, presents a less positive picture.

The two birthday poems to children, one for the Untermeyers'
son and the other for her niece, represent some of the worst features
of the form and, although singled out for praise by the *Literary
Digest*,[15] they are worth mentioning only for the way they seriously
undercut the value of motherhood. In each case the child is presented
not as the creation of the parents or the mother's nurturing, but
the result of the intervention of "angels":

> If an angel ever brings
> Me a baby in her wings,
> Please be certain that it grows
> Very, very much like Rose.
>   (*Rivers to the Sea*, 88)

Unlike the common view of the mother as the spiritual guide of her children, as in Lydia Sigourney's "A Father to His Motherless Children," these poems may in fact have been read as poems of praise to the glories of children, although they give no credit to the mother or motherhood. Motherhood is more seriously deprecated by the portrait of Mary, mother of Jesus, in the two poems about his life. A number of poets had written on this subject, stressing the human side of the Holy Family and Teasdale was certainly familiar with Josephine Peabody's "Canticle of the Babe." In Teasdale's poems Mary is disappointed by her son's lack of achievement and is portrayed as a simple housewife, upset that dinner will be cold because her son has stayed out too late and unable to comprehend the significance of his vocation.

The emphasis on this unimpressive view of motherhood is heightened by the placement of "The Mother of a Poet" immediately following these two. Written about Wheelock's mother, with whom Teasdale had become friendly and whom she visited many times, it is a paean of praise, finding "her soul as clear / and softly singing as an orchard spring's / In sheltered hollows all the sunny year." Although the mother treasures her infant as a "gift" and provides her son with "all he asked of earth and heaven," she is unable to understand his mature poetry "but in the end how many words / Winged on a flight she could not follow." She can only "be troubled by it, / The mother would soothe and set him free / Fearing the song's storm-shaken ecstasy." The attitude toward motherhood in all these poems seems to owe its substance to Teasdale's sense of her own mother's attitude toward her daughter, and they do not indicate any particular pleasure in the role. Unwilling to accept the staple of Victorian folk-wisdom that motherhood is the highest achievement of a woman's life, Teasdale seems not to imagine it to be a particularly rewarding experience.

Particular poems in this section are worthy of more careful consideration. "The Inn of Earth," a five-stanza ballad written in December 1911 and reflecting her early interest in medieval forms, may have been influenced by the Emily Dickinson poem #115, published in the 1891 edition as "What Inn Is This?" Teasdale's poem imagines life as a stopover on a journey at which the narrator asks for bread and wine and for a place to rest, only to be ignored by "the Host" who "went by with averted eye / And never a word said he." Seeking an alternative, the narrator tries to leave, but discovers that the host has "barred the outer door." Life, Teasdale is saying here, offers neither sustenance nor peace, yet there is no escape permitted by the forces in control, epitomized by the figure of the host.

Another form of disillusion is expressed in "The Star." A love affair between a star and its reflection in a pool is disturbed by a brown pig who "grunted and splashed and waded in," so muddying the waters that the image is lost. The poem was written to Eunice Tietjens, a woman whom she met during her trip to Chicago in 1913 and with whom she developed a friendship that was intense for a few years but continued throughout Teasdale's life. The star is specifically identified as "she" and the pool is one of Teasdale's most frequent images for a woman, suggesting that the love between the two women was threatened by some form of vulgarity. The difference between her response to this friendship as opposed to that she had known with Cummings is perhaps her reading of Kraft-Ebbing, who, while attempting to loosen the strictures of the Victorian morality, had also labeled homoerotic feelings as diseased.

The disillusion and pessimism of the section is, however, balanced by an opposing strand, not of optimism or faith, but of a growing strength and courage to accept life as it is. Various hints of it are interspersed throughout the section ("In Memoriam FOS," "Swallow Flight," "While I May"), but the conclusion provided by the last two poems makes the disillusionment worth the price it cost. In "Leaves" her faiths are identified with the leaves of a tree in autumn. Although the tree feels forsaken, there has been a compensation,

> But the little leaves that die
> Have left me room to see the sky;
> Now for the first time I know
> Stars above and earth below.
>   (*MH*, 24)

The clearer vision enables her to see both the heights (the stars) and the reality (the earth).

"The Answer" assumes a more assertive tone. Imagining the moment of her death, she foresees men who come with "false and feeble pity." In response to their emotion she declares:

> Be still, I am content,
> Take back your poor compassion,

> Joy was a flame in me
> Too steady to destroy;
> Lithe as a bending reed
> Loving the storm that sways her—
> I found more joy in sorrow
> Than you could find in joy.
>
> (*MH*, 23)

She does not pretend that life had been joyful, nor assume the optimistic tone that had been a staple of Victorian morality, but she is nonetheless affirmative, finding a value in the pains of life that were more valuable for her than pleasure is to most people. Together these two poems provide an additional answer to the questions posed in "Spring Night," which opened the volume—why does one continue to seek love as a source of meaning in life? The experience of emotion of any sort is worth the cost, she says here— for the insight one derives and for the sense of vitality that emotion provides. The independence of the tone is that of the New Woman, but it should be pointed out that Teasdale could imagine such boldness only at some point after death. She could move only a little distance beyond the world in which she had been reared.

Most of the poems in the next two sections were included in the original manuscript, but the new arrangement and the inclusion of a few new poems turns the relentlessly pessimistic tone of the original into a more sanguine view. Part 3, like the second section of Wheelock's manuscript, contains poems about the city, with the main thrust disappointments in love. The addition of "Testament" adds a corrective, however, for here the poet has gained a perspective by comparing her fate with that of all suffering humanity and accepts her suffering as part of the human condition. In her poetry notebook Teasdale had written an additional stanza that was wisely omitted from the final version, but its message reiterates the concluding poems of part 2—

> Give me, most awful God,
> Longing and pain and fears,
> If I shall see at last
> The clearer for my tears.
>
> (Poetry Notebook)

The long "From the Sea," written during her trip to Europe with
Jessie Rittenhouse, dominates part 4 and is a monologue in which
the speaker addresses a distant lover—he somewhere on shore, she
on board a ship. Like the monologue in *Helen,* it is lyrical rather
than dramatic, expressing emotions at a distance that the poet prefers
not to speak in her own voice, but the identification of narrator
with the poet is never questioned. The narrator imagines that the
lover stands next to her and asks him to appreciate the fact that
when they were together at some earlier time, she was "strong
enough to keep my love unuttered." While the poet accepts the
conventional role of the submissive Victorian woman when she says
"I longed to kneel to you that night," she breaks through those
bounds to add a description of the force of her passion: "In my heart
there was a beating storm. . . ." She asks the man to listen to
"my wistful, far-off singing touched with tears." Yet the conclusion
is more than sentimental melancholy; although the love will never
come to fruition, and although having "waked me," her lover "cannot give me sleep," nevertheless the memory has been worth it.
The conclusion joins the imagery of the sea to their walk together
on that memorable night:

> For us no starlight stilled the April fields,
> No birds awoke in darkling trees for us,
> Yet where we walked the city's street that night
> Felt in our feet the singing fire of spring,
> And in our path we left a trail of light
> Soft as the phosphorescence of the sea
> When night submerges in the vessel's wake
> A heaven of unborn evanescent stars.
>
> (*CP,* 80–82)

Their love is not only a source of joy to them, it is also a light for
others, and the poem is the harmony that puts the pain and pleasure
in balance.

The long poem to Sappho at the conclusion of the volume offers,
as discussed earlier, a concrete example of the interdependence of
love, beauty, and song. To the Sappho monologue published in
Helen of Troy Teasdale added two new segments, one of which had
been included in the Wheelock manuscript, the other created in
the intervening period. The new section of the Sappho monologue,

printed as the second of three parts, was written in May 1914, after she had met both Vachel Lindsay and Ernst Filsinger and was basking in the warmth of their attentions. In this poem Sappho is heard talking to a young girl who is a slave in Egypt, extolling first the power and beauty of the sea and then the joy and "precious pain" of love. Although Drake reads the poem as if Sappho were already dead and had found this love affair the end of life,[16] it may also be interpreted as the rescue from death by love, making the placement of the earlier monologue as the third part a more logical progression, that is, from weariness of life, and thoughts of death in part 1, to rescue through love in part 2, to fulfillment in motherhood in part 3. Its chief merit lies in the exquisite melodies it contains in the description of the sea:

> . . . can you think of fields
> Greater than Gods could till, more blue than night
> Sown over with the stars; and delicate
> With filmy nets of foam that come and go?
> It is more cruel and more compassionate
> Than harried earth. It takes with unconcern
> And quick forgetting, rapture of the rain
> And agony of thunder, the moon's white
> Soft-garmented virginity, and then
> The insatiable ardor of the sun.
>
> (*CP, 90*)

The extraordinary control that Teasdale now commanded over her medium is apparent in the easy flow of the lines while maintaining an absolute, strict ten-syllable count for each line, as the blank-verse form demanded.

When the volume was published in October 1915, it was both a popular and a critical success. But many contemporary readers enjoyed the "cute" poems like "The Look," which was widely parodied, or "Pierrot," with its echo of Austin Dobson, which jar modern critics, but the critics praised her skillful use of form, the "ecstasy that belongs to the wild sweet heart of song itself,"[17] and noted that "her brief, passionate, unfalteringly modelled lyrics [are] at once flame-like and sculpturesque. . . ."[18] And the public showed its appreciation by buying out edition after edition. At a period when interest in poetry had been stimulated by the discussions of the "new poetry" versus the traditional forms, Teasdale had seemingly combined elements of both strands by introducing modern settings for universal themes and placing them in beautifully wrought, traditional poetic forms. And at a time when some women were eagerly breaking out of the bonds of Victorian restraint, Teasdale's poetry could justify their claims to freedom yet soothe the less adventurous by her acceptance of traditional roles. To the world at large, she was the very personification of the New Woman who could combine career with marriage.

Chapter Six
Look to the Stars

The years between the publication of *Rivers to the Sea* and *Flame and Shadow* represent the period of Teasdale's greatest fame, during which she became one of the most popular poets in America with critical approbation that gave her a national reputation. At one point in 1917 she had three different volumes available: *Rivers to the Sea,* which had gone into its fourth printing; *The Answering Voice,* her anthology of women's love lyrics; and *Love Songs,* a collection of her own old and new poetry. Her poems were widely anthologized, translated into many different languages, and often set to music. She received national prizes for her work and herself served as judge for other awards. The facts of her life, however, present a scene of continuing illness and depression, of a marital relationship that was seriously flawed, and of a movement toward the withdrawal that was to cloud her later years. Nevertheless, she threw herself into work, undertaking a number of new projects, and while the quantity of new poems diminished, the quality took significant leaps forward. She no longer questioned her right to be a poet, and during these years she revised her relationship to her art from one of a debt to be paid to "a refuge for my spirit's sake, / A house of shining words" (*MH,* 31).

Even her technique was revised to produce sharper, more compressed images within a looser structure. And instead of the wistful melancholy of her earlier work, there is now a clear-eyed facing of the pains of life. Like Christina Rossetti, like her own image of Sappho, she envisaged the pain of life as the necessity for art. The ideas that emerge from the poems include a belief that she could achieve self-reliance by force of will alone, that she could face the storms of life without asking for pity. With ironic self-detachment she cataloged her torments in verse. The poems of this period reflect not simply the "loneliness of a woman beloved," as one critic has said, but the inescapable loneliness of life. [1]

The problems that Teasdale and her husband were facing in their marriage were carefully masked from the outside world, and she made every effort to present a view of the blissfully happy bride. One of her friends from her days with the Potters recalled a visit during the year they lived in St. Louis:

Ernest came in. Her whole face lighted up with joy, her sherry-brown eyes sparkled, she opened her arms wide, and he stooped to embrace her closely. I was a trifle embarrassed to be the witness of such a passionate love-scene, but Sara's gesture was perfectly spontaneous and natural.[2]

They also made an effort to find activities they could share, reading together and even writing poems together. Filsinger was well read and a lover of poetry, but he had little gift for verbal expression, and the venture soon died. "The Lighted Window" and "A Winter Bluejay" included in *Rivers* are among those recorded as joint efforts. Another instance where Teasdale put her husband's initial, as well as her own, at the end of a poem of joint authorship was "Song Making," which existed first as her own poem in the notebook, heavily revised and finally crossed out with the note "for improved version see 5 pages." But even the second copy with which Filsinger apparently helped her was changed yet again before its publication in the *Yale Review*. A few jointly written poems on pacifist themes grew out of their distaste for the World War. Filsinger's German heritage must have made the war difficult to accept, and Teasdale's antiwar feelings had probably developed during her years of friend-ship with Marion Cummings. Both were tolerant of a wide range of expression in print, regardless of their own particular tastes, and together they signed a petition organized by H. L. Mencken and addressed to the Postmaster General of the United States, protesting the banning of Theodore Dreiser's *The Genius*. They shared in Teas-dale's career, with Filsinger undertaking to read her poetry in public when she was too shy to do so herself. His obvious adoration of his wife and the mutual respect and affection they had for each other sustained the relationship during the first years of their marriage even though her severe infection with its excruciating pain meant separation, hospitalization, and finally a stay at Cromwell Hall. Equally, perhaps more important in keeping them apart were the long hours Filsinger spent at his work.

When the couple moved to New York, living, as in St. Louis, in residential hotels to spare Teasdale the trouble of running a home, they resumed their friendship with the literary group associated with the more progressive members of the Poetry Society and other like-minded poets, including Padraic Colum, Witter Brynner, E. L. Masters, Thomas Jones, William and Stephen Benét, Amy Lowell, Jessie Rittenhouse, Robert Frost, and, of course, John Wheelock. Among Teasdale's outings were visits, often with Wheelock as her escort, to Louis and Jean Untermeyer, who had "something a little bit like a salon."[3] She was particularly friendly with a group of women poets—Jean Starr Untermeyer, Aline Kilmer, Margaret Wilkinson, Margaret Widdemer—for whom she seemed, according to Wheelock, to have been a leader. But social events were strenuous for her and often left her exhausted owing to her extreme sensitivity, which was apparent to all who knew her. The joke in *Vanity Fair* about her sensitivity stemming from "having one layer of skin too few"[4] was based on a remark she made to a friend that a doctor in St. Louis had made just such a diagnosis.

The exact nature of Teasdale's physical and mental distress during these years is only partially known. In addition to the bladder infection, Jean Gould suggests that she had a miscarriage in 1915,[5] and Drake, with rather more reliable evidence, claims that she had an abortion in 1917.[6] The poem "Debt" with its lines "The wrong is done, the seed is sown, / The evil stands" is cited by Drake as indicating her response to her decision. Given the statements in her own letters about wanting to be a mother, about wanting to get married so that she could have children, and the evidence of her poetry that had frequently discussed the subject, such a decision must have been an agonizing one. The factors that governed it would have been her own frail health and the demands of her career. But it was not a decision that she, with her conventional upbringing and puritan values, could easily dismiss or forget. It may have also seriously affected her relationship with her husband, partly because of her sense of guilt, but also from the purely practical standpoint of avoiding intimacies as a way of avoiding further pregnancies.

Filsinger's new position required an immense amount of traveling, which would have put the major burden of parenthood on Teasdale, but his frequent absences during this period were in and of themselves a cause of her depression. Despite the tensions that existed while they were together, Teasdale relied heavily on her husband's support. He handled most of her ever-increasing mail; until 1917 he had read her poetry at public gatherings because she was too sensitive to do it herself; and he would, with Will Parrish's help, take care of all the details of publishing *The Answering Voice* while she retreated to Cromwell Hall. More important, she relied on his emotional support. Excitable though he was, given to sudden outbursts of anger over minor inconveniences, he nevertheless worshiped his wife, considered himself blessed to have married such a "rare and wonderful" woman, never criticized her or refused any request. He bolstered her always fragile sense of self-worth and, in his absence, Teasdale seemed more prone to lapse into morbidity. She might leave him for "rest-cures," as she did with increasing frequency, but when he left her she seems to have regarded it as a personal reproach.

In the first six months of 1918 alone Teasdale had gone off on five separate occasions to be by herself and recoup her flagging energies, finally going back for a month to the sanitarium in Connecticut. Filsinger continued to throw himself into his work and when the World War ended, prepared for extensive business trips, during 1919–20, first to Europe, then to South America, and, unexpectedly, back to Europe again, trips that kept them apart for almost a whole year. They had toyed with the notion of Teasdale accompanying him, but it is doubtful that either regarded it as a real possibility since she would never have managed the hectic schedule, the constant socializing, and the frequent moves from one uncomfortable hotel to another, for facilities in South America were often primitive and Europe was still recovering from the war's devastation. They did try one short trip together to Havana, Cuba, in December 1918, but the disruptions caused by a general strike made their stay an uncomfortable one. Even their brief period together between his first European trip and the one to South America was marred by a recurrence of her bladder inflammation and a respiratory infection.

Poetic Theory

The wide variety of experiments in poetry during these years had aroused considerable discussion over the merits of the new poetry versus the traditional forms. Teasdale's statements about poetry indicate that she was pondering the arguments being offered by proponents of the new poetry. While she was able to appreciate many of their contributions, she was more inclined to defend the traditional forms with which she worked. The significance of melody was more carefully spelled out, the need for sincerity stressed.

Curiously, even as she was publicly aligning herself in the camp of the traditionalists, she was privately experimenting with the newer forms. Teasdale stated her position first in an interview with her old friend from the Poetry Society, William Stanley Brathwaite, which was printed in the *Boston Evening Transcript* on 5 August 1916. Equating the interest in the new poetry with changing fashions, she quoted Robert Browning as saying the styles in music change every thirty years, then added:

The styles in poetry change just as often, and if melody is rare in the most fashionable kinds of poetry today, it is because it was over-prominent in the verse of thirty years ago. We are experiencing a reaction from Swinburne, Kipling, and many lesser men who employed highly elaborate metres and rhyme-schemes.[7]

In calling the new verse a reaction, however, she did not intend a total condemnation, for the poets have, she said, "emphasized the necessity for precision, compression and visualization, and they have infinitely enlarged the subject matter of poetry." What she did object to was the "tendency in some of the Imagists to dwell with a sort of self-conscious satisfaction on the frail and isolated beauties in nature or emotion. . . ."

What Teasdale prized in poetry was its ability to "deepen our sense of living" and "it makes little difference whether the poet accomplishes his object by the use of regular metre and rhyme or not." Perhaps even more important for her was the melody of poetry, and it is interesting to note the significance she attributed to it: ". . . melody seems to be so magical a thing. Indeed we must admit its magic because many lyrics that have little else besides melody have become priceless treasures of our race." It was here she cited Shakespeare's "Under the Greenwood Tree," mentioned earlier.

Traditional verse had an advantage that free verse lacked—"it is so easily remembered." The same idea was reiterated in a letter to her husband:

My main idea is that . . . poetry has to have a certain smooth-flowing quality in order to be easily memorized—and that to be easily memorized is one of the *reasons* for poetry. . . . One is absolutely forced to believe that the melody is in itself valuable—only valuable though . . . when it is unforced and fresh and inevitable.[8]

An interview, really a written statement to the newspapers, in 1918, elaborated her notions that the controversy over poetic forms was not the central issue:

If a poem is of any value it must spring directly from the experience of the writer—not necessarily from an external experience but at least from a spiritual one. If a poem is sincere and springs from deep emotion, no matter what the form, it will be of value to us.[9]

But the issue of poetic form continued to attract public attention and Teasdale could not stay out of the fray. She responded to Harriet Monroe's editorial in the March 1919 issue of *Poetry* on Max Eastman's conservative stance by writing a long letter intended for publication, withdrawing permission by telegram, however, immediately after mailing it to Chicago. In the letter she pointed to reliance of much of the "new poetry" on traditional, though foreign, poetry, which itself followed set standards for length of line and rhythms. She explained the modern poets' use of free verse "for the very good reason that they felt they can render what H. M. called 'the old pagan clarity' better in this way," but went on to justify metered verse. She praised the conventions, saying,

They enhance the fun of the game as the conventions enhance the fun of life. Could poetry be written conforming to more rigid laws, to take only one instance, than the Sapphics and the Alcaics of Sappho? . . . These fragments of hers have come down to us because the old grammarians preserved them as perfect examples of certain verse forms. No one would venture to say that Sappho would have written poetry more austerely beautiful if she had composed it in the complete freedom of vers libre.[10]

Again Teasdale was not here rejecting free verse, and she was careful to add, "No one could be more grateful than I, for the beauty they have given us in the new forms." The standard forms of poetry continued to be useful for Teasdale for their music and because the stanza by its very artifice and artificiality provided a distancing mechanism through which she could pour out her innermost thoughts without the sense of writing overpersonal confessions. She was aware, however, of the ways in which those forms could be inhibiting, describing the Poetry Society, their staunchest supporter, as a "hopeless place if one is expecting any spiritual awakening."[11]

Teasdale discussed her own sense of creativity in a statement she sent to Marguerite Wilkinson, who was preparing a book on modern poetry entitled *New Voices*. She placed central importance on the emotional aspect, saying: "My theory is that poems are written because of a state of emotional irritation. . . . The emotional irritation springs, probably, from subconscious combinations of partly forgotten thoughts and feelings."[12] The emotions may stem from actual or imaginary experience, both equally forceful, but "in either case the poem is written to free the poet from an emotional burden. Any poem not so written is only a piece of craftsmanship." The idea of a poem is, she felt, a light toward which the poet is groping and around which he walks, "so to speak, looking at it from all sides, trying to see which aspect of it is the most vivid. When he has hit upon what he believes is his peculiar angle of vision, the poem is fairly begun." The first line is crucial, setting the rhythm for the poem as a whole, and she describes it as "floating toward him with a charming definiteness of color and music."

Although she discounts the importance of form, which she says "should be engrossing neither to the poet nor to the reader," she does speak of the advantages of the traditional forms, which, being familiar, "carry the reader swiftly and easily to the heart of the poem. They do not astonish and bewilder him. Care needs to be taken to avoid dull and unconvincing sing-song." Brief lyrical poems need to be created in the poet's mind before being set down on paper and

In the process of molding his idea into a poem the poet will be at white heat of intellectual and emotional activity, bearing in mind that every word, every syllable, must be an unobtrusive and yet an indispensable part of his creation. Every beat of his rhythm, the color of each word, the ring of each rhyme must carry his poem, as a well-laid railway track carries a train of cars smoothly to its destination.[13]

The qualities that Teasdale singled out as dangers—"the amazing word, the facile inversion, the clever twist of thought"—were among those features that were being regarded as values. It was just such strictures that would prevent her from a more total commitment to the new poetry. Yet she was not against the idea that a poem might be thought-provoking, for though she believed that the "reader must be left free to feel and not think while he is reading a poem," she added, "the thinking should come afterward."

Teasdale's appreciation of what was happening in poetry was a limited one, and she was unaware of the demand for psychological probing and intellectual rigor that was to dominate poetry for many years. She could not foresee that the increased compression that would turn a poem, as she had written to Page some years before, from a "flower" into a "nut" would soon become a value, not a fault. Nor could she foresee how the "change in styles" would leave her own poetry ignored by serious critics. In many respects she had already adopted some of the standards that were being enunciated; her own poetry was increasingly precise in its word choice, its tendency to wordiness had been tamed, and more attention was being paid to creating an objectification of emotion. And certainly she had been among the first to enlarge the subject matter of poetry. Now she was to embark on other changes. But the one virtue of traditional poetry that Teasdale could not abandon and that prevented more serious excursions into free verse was her concern for melody. The words she used in the interview with Brathwaite to talk about it are significant—it was magic. Her almost primitive response to the incantatory power of song provides much of the power of her better work.

Teasdale's defense of her own method of creation did not interfere with her appreciation of many of the volumes of new poetry that were being published, and the opportunity to prove her open-mindedness came when she was asked to serve as one of the three judges for the poetry prize in 1918. Although the choice was theoretically limited to nominated volumes, she read all the major volumes of poetry published for the year and arranged the nomination of the one she preferred. Her first choice was Carl Sandburg's *Cornhuskers,* which she felt was head and shoulders above the rest, although she also liked works by E. L. Masters, Conrad Aiken, and Lola Ridge.[14] Her two fellow judges, Professors William Lyons Phelps and Richard Burton, she was shocked to discover, had ruled out all free verse, and it took all her powers of persuasion to get them to agree to make a joint award to Sandburg along with their selection, Margaret Widdemer. Widdemer's poetry was a typical example of what Emily Stipes Watt's identifies as the "female lyricist"[15]—the small, neat, dainty lyrics, the tone of wistful melancholy, a sense of imagery for decorative purposes, coupled with deft craftsmanship. To this category Teasdale, Millay, Wylie, and Reese are still frequently and erroneously assigned.

The Answering Voice

Teasdale's next project brought her to the forefront of those concerned with feminist issues at the time even as it placed her with the supporters of traditional verse. She had spent most of the first year of her marriage putting together *Rivers to the Sea* and because of its huge success her publisher was anxious to bring out another volume of her work, but there were too few new poems for such a purpose. She had continued to write, but at a slower pace and fewer of the finished works seemed worth publication. As a substitute, Teasdale suggested an anthology of women's love poems. While she had frequently derided the radical women's militancy and had avoided any unconventional freedoms herself, she nonetheless was aware of the problems women faced and was anxious to solidify their position as artists. She seems also to have planned an article on women poets, for the flyleaf of one of her poetry notebooks lists several names for that purpose. Her acceptance by the established poets after her first visit to New York may have momentarily blurred this issue, but her awareness of the difference between her ideal view of marriage and her actual experience of it may have brought home to her the need to reassess other women's responses to love.

Just one hundred poems would be included. Since she was still living in St. Louis at the time and was in poor health, her husband and her sister Mamie, to whom the book was dedicated, brought books to her sickbed and numerous literary friends were solicited for possible inclusions, with the title suggested by John Wheelock. The goals that she wished to achieve in this anthology were stated, in part, in the one-page introduction she wrote, noting that before the nineteenth century ". . . for reasons well known to the student of feminism, sincere love poems by women were very rare in England and America," but that "since the middle of the last century, the works of women have compared favorably with that of men. . . ." Because "the finest utterance of women's hopes has been on love," her aim was to produce, alluding to Palgrave's anthology, a "golden treasury of lyrics by women."[16]

Many of the poets she included are still highly respected today: she used five poems by Elizabeth Barrett Browning and five by Christina Rossetti, two by Emily Dickinson (in versions available at that time, which seriously distort their real meaning), and one by Edna St. Vincent Millay. She also included works by fine poets such as Lizette Woodworth Reese, Louise Imogen Guiney, Anna Hempstead Branch, and Ella Wilcox Wheeler, whose reputations have been obscured by the radical shift in poetic taste that marked the first half of the twentieth century. Her sense of good manners and shrewd politics may have been responsible for the inclusion of poems by three friends from the Potters group, three poems by Zoë Akins, and works by new friends who were influential in her career— Jessie Rittenhouse, Harriet Monroe, Amy Lowell, Marguerite Wilkinson, and Margaret Widdemer. Four poems by her childhood favorite, A. Mary F. Robinson, as well as a number of forgotten poets, filled out the volume.

From the poems in the anthology it is clear that the music of the verses is the most outstanding common denominator. Purity of intent rather than tension or ambiguity was preferred, and images from nature dominate, with the pain of unfulfilled love the general theme. Resignation or death are seen as the only alternatives to this unhappy state. The poems, in fact, sum up the conventional women's view with all the melancholy, submissiveness, girlish coquettishness, death-haunted love that distinguished almost all of women's love poems at that time. The frequency of bird images and of sanctuaries affirms Cheryl Walker's thesis that these were the only escapes that most women could find from their sense of entrapment.[17]

As a whole, the volume stands as a testament to all the standards of poetry by women that Teasdale herself was outgrowing. It is as if the preparation of this volume had led Teasdale to evaluate the poetry of women and to find it inadequate to her needs. The anthology was nevertheless popular, and while most reviewers noted its "charm and beauty,"[18] others were less charitable. Conrad Aiken complained that it did not show "what a woman really thinks,"[19] expecting, perhaps, the bolder statements that were only then in the process of being written. But if modern readers are disappointed, it should be noted that, as Drake points out, Teasdale was "the first to compile an anthology setting forth a coherent picture of women's attitudes toward love."[20] It gave the older generation a sense of what their experience had been, and it gave the new generation an idea of how their own perceptions might reassess the view of a woman's world and her feelings.

Love Songs

Teasdale was anxious also to bring out another volume of her own poetry, but she found very few of her new poems worthy of reprinting. Her notebooks show that she was embarking on a number of false paths. On two occasions she wrote poems for specific situations—one an ode on Shakespeare's mother for the Drama Guild of St. Louis's commemoration of the tercentenary of Shakespeare's death; the other, on the same theme requested by William Stanley Brathwaite, for a similar occasion in Boston. Disappointed with both efforts, she vowed never to write poetry to order again. But even on her own she seems to have had difficulty finding a form for her feelings. On one occasion she wrote a long, gory, balladlike poem about St. Kevin, who threw a woman off the cliffs because she tempted him to be untrue to his vows of celibacy; at other times she tried out poems about an old man, about the ships in the harbor at Charlevoix, about Newark, New Jersey. Not only were there many poor pieces, but also her own critical attitude toward her poetry had sharpened. To make a complete volume, she decided to reprint the best of her earlier work for a book entitled *Love Songs*. Of the approximately seventy-five poems she wrote between 1915 and 1917, less than twenty were considered worthy for this new book, although quite a few later found their way into *Flame and Shadow*. It was the most successful volume she ever published, the first edition selling out in only two months and six editions published within a year. It also received the first national poetry prize ever awarded, the Columbia Poetry Prize, a precursor of the Pulitzer Prize for Poetry, which had been omitted when those prizes were first conceived.

The inclusion of so many early poems with the new creations has masked the significant steps forward that Teasdale had been making, which can be seen particularly in one group of poems, published as a unit called "Songs of Sorrow." They form a true poetic unity, the fruit of her struggle to achieve a larger structure for her work. Her previous attempts had been to group poems by form in her first two books, or by a narrative structure in the first part of *Rivers*, or by particular images—the city and the sea—to unify other sections.

In "Songs out of Sorrow" the unity is provided by a single metaphor transformed from earthbound to spiritual significance. Written for the most part during the summer of 1916 when she was at Cromwell Hall, they present a serious reappraisal of her life similar to the one she had made after her visit with Marion Cummings Stanley—the need to be self-reliant, to find within herself the strength and reason to live. The opening poem, "Spirit's House," announces the poet's determination to make use of the pain of life:

> From naked stones of agony
> I will build a house for me;
> As a mason all alone
> I will raise it, stone by stone,
> And every stone where I have bled
> Will show a sign of dusky red.
> I have not gone the way in vain,
> For I have good of all my pain;
> My spirit's quiet house will be
> Built of naked stones I trod
> On roads where I lost sight of God.
>   (*MH*, 34)

Its theme is like Rossetti's in "From House to Home" which described a woman who "measured measureless sorrow towards its length, and breadth and depth and height" and who could endure and create song from the experience, suggesting that "for the woman poet only renunciation or even anguish, can be a suitable source of song."[21] In Teasdale's poem these stones of agony become the substitute sanctuary to replace her former belief in God. It is the very pain of loss of faith that will become her refuge.

The self-reliance is carried forward in the next two poems, "Mastery" and "Lessons." In "Mastery" the poet says

> I would not have a god come in
> To shield me suddenly from sin
> And set my house of life to rights.
>   (*MH*, 33)

Knowing how frequently the word *god* has been used in her poems for husband or lover, the poem clearly marks her declaration of independence. As a poem of a married woman, it is in marked contrast to the traditional image of the wife's dependence on her husband that Teasdale, and many women of her generation, had accepted. If in "Mastery" she rejects the help of those stronger than herself, in "Lessons" she realizes the futility of seeking help from those weaker. She must learn "to seek no strength in waving reeds / Nor shade beneath a straggling pine."

The cost of such an attitude is not belittled. In the next poem, "Wisdom," she notes that cost, once she gives up complaints about the imperfections of life and accepts compromise.

> When I have ceased to break my wings
> Against the faultiness of things,
> And learned that compromises wait
> Behind each hardly opened gate,
> When I can look Life in the eyes,
> Grown calm and very coldly wise,
> Life will have given me the Truth
> And taken in exchange—my youth.
>
> (*MH, 33*)

Not only life but also death must be faced, and in "In a Burying Ground" the poet imagines that her body will be the source of flower's beauty, a reflection of the Whitmanesque image of grass as "the beautiful uncut hair of graves." The image of beauty unites this poem with the next, "Wood Song," in which the poet hears a bird song composed of just three notes. Inspired by the wood thrush's ability and willingness to create beauty with the limited resources at its disposal, she exclaims, "I caught life back against my breast / And kissed it, scars and all." Now the poet looks back at the "stones of agony" of the first poem and finds new meaning—her refuge is in her art—

> From my spirit's gray defeat,
> From my pulse's flagging beat,
> From my hopes that turned to sand,
> Sifting through my close-clenched hand,
> From my own fault's slavery,
> If can sing, I still am free.
>
> For with my singing I can make
> A refuge of my spirit's sake,

A house of shining words, to be
My fragile immortality.

(*MH*, 31)

The house of stone has become a house of song.

While the sequence may be too preachy for modern ears, if it is too insistent on the power of the will to overcome difficulties, it does represent a significant step forward for Teasdale as a woman in its rejection of the submissive wife, rejecting sentimentality, praising strength, power over the self, and as a poet determined to use her art in more significant ways.

The simplicity of the "Songs out of Sorrow" is countered by the more complex tone of the poem Teasdale used to open the volume. "Barter" is one of her most popular poems, but its underlying tension is often missed.

> Life has loveliness to sell,
>   And beautiful and splendid things,
> Blue waves whitened on a cliff,
>   Soaring fire that sways and sings,
> And children's faces looking up
> Holding wonder like a cup.
>
> Life has loveliness to sell,
>   Music like a curve of gold,
> Scent of pine trees in the rain
>   Eyes that love you, arms that hold,
> And for your spirit's still delight,
> Holy thoughts that star the night.
>
> Spend all you have for loveliness,
>   Buy it and never count the cost;
> For one white singing hour of peace
>   Count many a year of strife well lost,
> And for a breath of ecstasy
> Give all you have been, or could be.
>
> (*MH*, 29)

The poem extols the pleasures of living. The basic metaphor is of a market transaction, a feature more strongly apparent in an earlier version copied in her notebook. There it was entitled "Buying

Loveliness" and the first line of the second stanza was "Life will not give but she will sell."[22] Most of the poem recounts moments of beauty with such rich imagery that it is easy to forget there is a price to pay—sights full of color, sounds, scents, tactile sensations, the physical joys producing spiritual contentment. And the cost, stated in the last four lines, is presented in such a straightforward way that it is easy to lose sight of how expensive it is. One hour of peace may demand years of pain; a breath of ecstasy, no longer than a moment or two, may cost all one's past or future. The tone is not rueful or bitter; the proposition is no more sentimental than any business deal. The ironic note is understood only after one reflects on the poem.

In the other new poems in the volume Teasdale makes a few interesting and somewhat different notes about love. There is a plea for a more passionate lover and the awareness of the waywardness of her affections. As poems written by a married woman, they suggest a serious revision of the conventional attitude. It is as if she had found that the accepted image of the wife did not fit the facts of an intelligent, passionate woman's spirit. The desire for a more passionate relation is masked in "Because," but it is nonetheless there. Written while Ernst was on a business trip, it seems to praise him for his gentleness and consideration, "Oh, because you never tried / To bow my will or break my pride, / And nothing of the caveman made. . . ." But then it goes on to say, "Take me." Repeated three times, the imperative "take" seems as if the poet is pleading with her lover to be more aggressive. Although she was married, she was aware, as she wrote in "Doubts," that she could only guarantee the fidelity of her body, but not her soul, which was "a wild, gay adventurer; / A restless and eager wraith" that might break "faith with you." In "The Wind" she acknowledges the limits of love: "There is no peace for me on earth, / Even with you." Instead of inspiring her to new creativity, she found that marriage was stultifying. In "House of Dreams" she compliments her husband for fulfilling all her dreams but goes on to say that "the empty dreams were dim, / And the empty dreams were wide" and now they have come true, her "thoughts have no place now to play / And nothing now to do" (*CP,* 107–8). Even her sense of creativity has been crushed. In "Tree of Song" she announces that she cannot write poems to her husband. "I sang my songs for the rest, / For you, I am still . . . / The tree of song stands bare" (*CP,* 106).

Where a love relationship is mentioned, it is often about a remembered one, as in "Spring Rains" or "The Ghost" or "Jewels," in which her memories are like the jewels women put away "and cannot wear in sober day," that is, in the reality of her new situation as a married woman.

The long monologue with which the volume ends harks back to her days in New York before her marriage, and in its opening goes back farther still to the medieval fairy-tale images of her days in St. Louis, which show her merging memory and imagination into dream. Like a king and queen, the narrator and her lover sit on the top of one of the old two-story buses that used to travel up and down Fifth Avenue and "watch our subjects with a naughty joy." Reaching the park, they walk through the wintry landscape, imagining a fairy ring around the bench on which they once sat, recalling former scenes and admiring the stars' reflections in the lake. As they walk, however, the mists gather, "the curtain of fog / Making it strange to all the friendly trees." Even her companion grows strange and far as he walks ahead of her, and at the end she imagines the park as theirs alone, "We are alone now in a fleecy world; / Even the stars have gone. / We two alone!" (*CP,* 110–12). While it is tempting to speculate whether the poet-lover is Lindsay or Wheelock, the atmosphere of the poem suggests that the man is as much an imaginary character in the dream that Teasdale has created from bits of reality.

Several poems do speak of her happiness with her husband, such as "Dew," "Thought," and "Riches," but the preponderant message is one of protest, confusion, doubt about the role she is expected to play or the emotions she is expected to feel. Teasdale had been more honest in these poems than she had ever been before, but she had found a convenient mask in burying them with her other, more lighthearted, poems.

Flame and Shadow

The culmination of this five-year period came with the publication of a new collection of poems, *Flame and Shadow,* in 1920. The changes in theme, technique, and attitude that were developing over these years are increasingly apparent in this new volume.

In part, Teasdale's new approach may have stemmed from her reading during this period, which is interesting for certain changes it reveals. Just before her marriage she had read all of the three volumes of Emily Dickinson then available, and two volumes of Frost's, adding the third in the next year. In addition to reading the new works by her friends, she also started to read critical works such as Van Wyck Brook's *America's Coming of Age*, Lowell's *Tendencies in Modern American Poetry*, as well as a number of novels by Henry James and James Joyce's *Portrait of the Artist as a Young Man*. An unusual book on her list is Evelyn Underhill's *Practical Mysticism*.

Yeats's poetry, however, became her favorite. She had heard him speak in New York in 1914, and again in 1919 in Santa Barbara, and his name appears frequently in her reading notebook during these years. She wrote Harriet Monroe, "I have been reading Yeats furiously again. He is the greatest living poet without the shadow of a doubt."[23] Her appreciation of Yeats was stressed again when, in answer to a request from the librarian of a small college in Missouri, she supplied a list of modern poets that might be included in their collection. In addition to mentioning Frost, Robinson, Sandburg, Aiken, Markham, and Dickinson, "the most gifted woman poet America has ever had," she added, "I should buy everything of W. B. Yeats' at the very first. He is the supreme artist writing in our tongue today."[24] When she saw the librarian's final selection and noted that Yeats's *Wild Swans at Coole* had been omitted, she sent him a copy of it. Teasdale also had the opportunity of meeting Yeats when he lectured in Santa Barbara, where she had gone for the winter of 1919–20 while her husband was on his extended business trip. Yeats's poetic career had traced many of the same paths as Teasdale's, from the hazy medievalism of the late nineteenth century to the sharper, more natural diction with an emphasis on the expression of the poet's sensibility rather than concern with moral uplift and preachiness. And unlike many of the other modern poets, Yeats had retained the primacy of melody in his verse.

One of the major effects of reading Yeats, as well as other modern poets, was the change in technique that appears for the first time in the poems in *Flame and Shadow*. Amy Lowell, in a congratulatory letter on the appearance of the poem "Places" in the June 1919 issue of *Scribner's* said, "The effect you get by your non-scanable metrical lines is perfectly charming. I remember your telling me in New York that you were experimenting in this sort of thing, and I want to tell you that I think your experiment is highly successful."[25] While that poem might seem, to modern readers, quite regular, the lines varying no more than one or two syllables from the standard twelve-beat measure established in the opening, it represents a significant shift from the absolute precision that had marked her earlier work. A more obvious example of the new approach is one of her best loved poems, "Let It Be Forgotten."

> Let it be forgotten, as a flower is forgotten,
>   Forgotten as a fire that once was singing gold,
> Let it be forgotten for ever and ever,
>   Time is a kind friend, he will make us old.
>
> If anyone asks, say it was forgotten
>   Long and long ago,
> As a flower, as a fire, as a hushed footfall
>   In a long forgotten snow.
>
>   (MH, 62)

The poem, she had written Eunice Tietjens, "was written almost entirely without intervention by my brains. It simply was in my mind. But I was broad awake all the time and could not be said to be in a subconscious state."[26] The poem owes much to one by A. Mary F. Robinson that had been included in The Answering Voice. A comparison between the two reveals how far Teasdale had surpassed her early favorite:

> **Rispetto**
>
> II
>
> Let us forget we love each other much,
>   Let us forget we ever had to part,
> Let us forget that any look or touch
>   Once let in either to the other's heart.
>
> Only we'll sit upon the daisied grass
>   And hear the larks and see the swallows pass;
> Only we'll live awhile, as children play,
>   Without to-morrow, without yesterday.[27]

Robinson's poem, reflecting the carpe diem theme, is a charming plea for enjoyment of the moment. The images of the "daisied grass" and the flying birds are pleasant enough, but they add nothing to the depth of the thought, and the repeated "Let us forget" with its slightly rueful tone, somewhat clashes with the call to pleasure that is the main substance of the verse.

For Teasdale, the opening phrase assumes greater significance, controlling the whole poem. By changing the verb tense, Teasdale has moved it from a simple suggestion to complex advice. The phrase "let it be forgotten" implies the existence of events that, having happened some time in the past, continue to plague the mind, and each item she lists becomes a symbol of just such moments—the flower, the remembrance of a love affair; the fire, the warmth and beauty of a passion; the snow, the cold sterility after love has gone. The harshness of the last line of the first stanza cuts through the threatened sentimentality with its blunt reminder that old age brings dimmer mental powers, its dissonance clashing with the smooth harmony of the preceding lines. But the power of the poem lies also in the shrewd use of psychology. The insistent pounding of the word *forgotten* plays on the mind's tendency to store concepts in groups of opposites. Hearing "forgotten," the reader will also hear the echoing "remember." And if the memories were not so strong, there would be no need to insist on forgetting; in fact, each line, instead of aiding in the process of eliminating the thoughts, conjures up all the associations that might collect around a particular flower, a special fire. And the final image, with its allusion to a poem by François Villon unforgotten after six centuries—"Ou sont les nieges d'antan?" (Where are the snows of yesterday?)—underlines the contradictions in the message; in insisting on forgetfulness, the poem actually strengthens memory.

The poem is also a technical tour de force. The chantlike quality of the repeated opening phrase is heightened by the use of the word *forgotten* six times in eight lines, yet monotony is avoided by the careful placement of the word within each of the lines. The first time it is used it is given its usual pronunciation with the stress on the second syllable, the next time, in the same line, it receives a strong secondary stress on the last syllable. In the last line equal stress is given to all three syllables. The varying length of the lines reveals Teasdale's skill with her new form. Instead of measuring her lines by the number of syllables in each, she is now measuring them by the number of stressed syllables—there are three stresses per line, while the syllable count varies from fourteen in the first to a mere five in the sixth. Yet the poem retains the same melodic harmony that was always Teasdale's basic requirement for her "songs."

In moving away from metrical regularity Teasdale was adopting the chanted cadences from the earliest sources of poetry, rather than re-creating the rhythmic patterns of natural speech, which Frost, for instance, was in the process of developing. But the verbal insistence on forgetting coupled with the implied remembering provides the perfectly balanced opposition that make this one of Teasdale's finest achievements.

In organizing the poems for *Flame and Shadow* Teasdale was working toward a new sense of cohesiveness within the volume, the balancing of opposites providing the basic structure. The arrangement of the poems, she wrote her husband, "will serve to show that the many short poems are in reality one life poem, or parts of it. I have managed it so that each poem has congenial companions on either side of it."[28] The title, derived from a line of Victor Hugo's, used as the epigraph, "Recois la flamme ou l'ombre / De tous mes jours" (Remember the flame or the shadow all my days) enunciates the pattern. But the meanings given to the two key images vary and the distinctions are not always clear. In the first section *Flame* represents the brightness of life, while in section 2, "Memories," *Shadow* is the dimmer light of recollection. Thereafter, the images of light and dark are mingled within the sections. Section 3, which is chiefly centered around her husband, considers both the brightness and darkness of married love, while section 4, "In a Hospital," considers the darkness of physical pain and the new flashes of light she finds from it. The pain of memory, its darker side, dominates section 5, the poems concerned mainly with her feelings for Wheelock, yet some brightness is treasured. Thoughts of death in "The Dark Cup" bring forth both sorrow and wisdom that are its "flame and shadow." In section 6, the poet contrasts the value and cost of her lonely communion with nature, while section 7 considers those factors that dim human perception, ending with a poem in praise of "Lovely Chance." In section 8 the darkness and destruction of war stand against the eternal renewal of nature. In "By the Sea," section 9, the unending power of the sea brings forth both negative and positive feelings. The value and difficulties of the solitary life are considered in section 10, while section 11, the least clear of all, reflects on the sad effects of change that are visible versus other unchanging, but hidden values. The last section, "Songs for Myself," affirms the value of the self with its ability to accept the mixed quality of life, bringing back the flame of the title.

The opening poem of the first section, "Blue Squills," sets the tone not only for the first section but for the entire volume, in its contrast between the beauty of spring and the inevitability of death. By placing her own life as only a moment within the eons of life on earth—

> How many million Aprils came
> Before I ever knew
> How white a cherry bough could be,
> A bed of squills, how blue.

she captures the fleetingness of her perception of beauty. With this knowledge she pleads,

> Oh burn me with your beauty,
> . . . Wound me, that I, through endless sleep
> May bear the scar of you.
>
> *(MH*, 48)

The "flame" of beauty and the "shadow" of the pain from the intensity of her response can together provide a kind of immortality. Other sources of brightness are detailed in the section in addition to the beauties of the earth—the beauty of the skies, the knowledge of her own strengths, of song, the feelings of passion, even the rest that death might bring.

One of the joys detailed in this opening, the power of "song," and of sound in general, is examined throughout the book in close detail. In the opening it is both extolled in "Meadowlarks" as "the white flying joy when a song is born" yet limited to being a minor part of herself in "What Do I Care?," the poem written in response to Untermeyer's criticism that her poems do not show her intelligence.[29] Music is the medium for her memories in "Places," where "places I love come back to me like music" and the sounds of the ship's engine and the man's voice "speaking, hushed, insistent, / At midnight, in mid-ocean, hour on hour to me" preserve the memory. In the same way the "Redbirds" bring back the memories of her visits to Saxton's Hill, the place outside St. Louis she had explored with her friends in her youth. The sounds of the wind carry the voice of her lover. But it is her own power to create song that provides joy, best expressed in "Compensation,"

> I should be glad of loneliness
> And hours that go on broken wings,
> A thirsty body, a tired heart
> And the unchanging ache of things,
> If I could make a single song
> As lovely and as full as light,
> As hushed and brief as a falling star
> On a winter night.
>
> (*MH*, 63)

But song has its limitations. In "The Net" it fails to capture the special qualities of her lover, "I made you many and many a song, / Yet never one told all you are." Nor does she feel that her gift of poetry is within her control; like the ripe fruit on a tree in "My Heart is Heavy," she feels that "my songs do not belong to me." Although she has known "the deep solace of song" ("The Dreams of My Heart") yet it is as short-lived as "the bright frailty of foam" ("A Little While").

Far more disturbing is her realization in "In Spring, Santa Barbara" that pain is a necessity for creating her poems and that despite the happiness she feels at the prospect of her lover's return, "I have been as still as stone, / My heart sings only when it breaks." If that is so, however, then song can become a value, for with it she can "like barley bending . . . / rise from pain" and, "change my sorrow / Into song." Further, her poetry has the value of providing a kind of immortality, as in the poem "It Will Not Change," originally entitled "Love," where "It will live on / In all my songs for you / When I am gone." But the cost is high, as she explains in "Song Making": "I had to take my own cries / And thread them into a song."[30] It is the price that she must pay for having lived— "But oh, the debt is terrible, / That must be paid in song."

The place of song, her sense of herself as a creative artist, has changed from the sense of being the "refuge" that it had been in *Rivers to the Sea*, to a debt. She has rationalized her right to be a poet and no longer is concerned about the propriety of her decision to have a career as she had been in her earlier books. In fact, she feels her ability to create is outside her control. But while the gift of poetry was in the "Sappho" poems a debt incurred in exchange for life and love, it is now a debt exchanged for life alone.

The love that she had dreamed of had not materialized. And it is precisely the failure of that kind of love that these poems document. That failure may have been due to the nature of her husband's love; his adoration of her as a "rare and wonderful" goddess placed her on a pedestal that might have inhibited normal human affection. Or the failure may have been due to Filsinger's lack of passion. Teasdale's puritanical background has frequently been cited as a causative factor and it is certainly true that few if any human relationships could have lived up to her over-idealized expectations. In *Rivers to the Sea* she had expressed the belief that love would provide the inspiration necessary for the perception of "Beauty" and for the transmutation of beauty into poetry. Now she realized that love had failed.

A main point in this book is to question the position of women in marriage. Although in "Driftwood" she says one of the flames of her life has come from "my lovers . . . who gave the flame its changeful / and iridescent fires," she decries the submissiveness that the married state demands of women in "Oh You Are Coming." In that poem she is not afraid to say, "Are not my thoughts clearer than your thoughts / And colored like stones in a running stream?"— suggesting her belief that her intellect was equal to any man's, yet the independence that she feels entitled to is denied: "Oh why must I lose myself to love you, / My dear?" She does not deny the joy of love; she cries, "He is home, he is here / In the whole world no other / Is dear as my dear!" But in "The Mystery" she is aware of their separateness:

> But when we look
>   At each other so
> Then we feel
>   How little we know;
>
> The spirit eludes us,
>   Timid and free—
> Can I ever know you
>   Or you know me?
>   (*MH*, 52)

The lover's coming in "Eight O'Clock" may break the monotony of her hospital stay, but there is no sense that he can spare her pain. Passion itself is limited in "Spring Torrents," where she feels herself "like a rock that knows the cry of waters / And cannot answer at all." It is the memory of a lost love rather than the fulfilled one that provides the inspiration that creates her poetry, those memories "Deep in my heart they lie, / hidden in their splendor, / Buried like sovereigns in their robes of state." But even there, the poet would not have her memories challenged by reality:

> Let them not awake again, better to lie there,
>   Wrapped in memories, jewelled and arrayed—
> Many a ghostly king has waked from death sleep
> And found his crown stolen and his throne decayed.
>   (*MH*, 44)

If love fulfilled is inadequate and memory of lost love dangerously insubstantial, where then does a woman find her strength and a woman poet find the inspiration to transmute beauty into song? The first answer comes in the center of the book, in a poem entitled "The Dark Cup." Five of the eight poems of this group were published originally in *Contemporary Verse* and received the award as the best work published in that magazine for 1920. The cup to which she refers is the cup of death, the image perhaps referring to the cup of hemlock that was presented to Socrates, about whom she had been reading during these years. But it is also the awareness of death that is the motive for making the most of life. In "Since There is no Escape" she says,

> Let me go down as waves swept to the shore
> In pride; and let me sing with my last breath;
> In these few hours of light I lift my heart;
> Life is my lover—
>   (*Flame and Shadow*, 67)

She hopes in "The Wine" that she might find "some shining strange escape" because she "sought in Beauty the bright wine of immortality." A proud spirit defying death by asserting her love of life, she treasures the sensations she receives from the physical world even as she acknowledges its ugly aspects and the inevitability of death in "In a Cuban Garden" and even insists on a kind of life after death in which she and her lover will exist "beyond living, beyond dying, / Knowing and known unchangeable." Her love of life is expressed in "June Night," in a love of the physical beauty of the world. Thoughts of the lost love do not disappear; they serve only to accentuate the solitude of the poet in "I Thought of You" or turn out to be illusions in "In the End."

Having chosen to replace love as the prime motive for life and art, Teasdale then chooses to replace the lover with the self, relying on its own ability to communicate with the natural world. In the unreality of a fog-shrouded world she reassures herself:

> Here in a world without a sky,
> Without the ground, without the sea,
> The one unchanging this is I
> Myself remains to comfort me.
> ("White Fog," *CP*, 139)

She finds a communion with ancient Greece through the shining of stars ("Arcturus"), expects that age will diminish the pain of unfulfilled passion ("Moonlight"), and although she knows that she may be lonely, she exclaims, "Only the lonely are free" ("Morning Song"). Fears of old age and death do not disappear, but she can praise "Lovely Chance" that has kept her whole. The failure of all mankind is encapsulated in the group of poems on the viciousness and hate of war from which the poet finds solace in the indifference of nature and in the "faithful beauty of the stars" ("Winter Stars"). Memories of the lover keep her company and suggest the possibility of some meeting after death, but it is her own thoughts that are her best companions: "When I am all alone / Envy me then, / For I have better friends / Than women and men" ("Thoughts"). People, in fact, are difficult to be with, even on a city street because she "cannot bear / The sorrow of the passing faces" ("Faces") or the possibility that they may see hers. Aware that no one knows "another's heartbreak" and that death might be a release from pain, in the poem written in memory of her brother who died at the age of forty-seven after suffering from a stroke ("The Silent Battle"), she sees the self, "my innermost Me," as the sanctuary that would give her the strength to accept life. But that self must give up love and hate, detach itself from the suffering of humanity, and even refuse the solace of prayer ("The Sanctuary"). Not always able to pay such a price, she is aware of "fear an unhealing wound in my breast" ("At Sea").

The affirmation of the self finds its culmination in the last section, entitled "Songs for Myself." The image of the unself-conscious tree represents the goal she seeks ("The Tree"), and all the achievements of life she has struggled so hard to attain have turned out to be hollow: "Even love . . . / And music and men's praise and even laughter / Are not so good as rest" ("At Midnight"). Poetry has demanded too high a price ("Song Making"); at times her loneliness seems too great to bear with only her "own spirit's pride" to keep her "from the peace of those / Who are not lonely, having died" ("Alone"). She fears the return of desire ("Red Maples") yet her pride asserts itself in "Debtor" and she declares that

> So long as my spirit still
> Is glad of breath . . .
> How can I quarrel with fate
> Since I can see
> I am a debtor to life,
> Not life to me?
>
> (*MH*, 39)

The final poem, "Wind in the Hemlock," provides a summation, as Drake has pointed out,[31] of the major theme of the volume. The opening two sections of this forty-line poem describe the night skies. No longer images of purity or divinity, she calls them "steely stars and moon of brass," the metallic quality suggesting the machinelike world that mocks her mortality.

> You know as well as I how soon
> I shall be blind to stars and mood,
> Deaf to the wind in the hemlock tree,
> Dumb when the brown earth weighs on me.
>
> (*MH*, 49–50)

She rages against the inevitability of death, seeing man as its slave, earth as a malign force "impatient for him since his birth." These two stanzas show the failure of any item of nature as a reassurance, or source of comfort, or hope. Moving from these images in which she had previously found spiritual sustenance, she turns now to the tree. It is fragrant, it sings as the wind blows through it, it shelters the birds, and, most significantly, it knows neither anger nor doubt nor envy. From the serenity she finds in the hemlock, the poet derives the following message:

> If I am peaceful, I shall see
> Beauty's face continually:
> Feeding on her wine and bread
> I shall be wholly comforted,
> For she can make one day for me
> Rich as my lost eternity.

Beauty, the replacement for her lost religion, as the mention of "wine and bread" indicates, is available now only when she, like the hemlock, can achieve total acceptance of her mortal state. Love no longer functions as the catalyst. The lone tree, isolate, uncomplaining, is in its endurance able to nurture forces within itself that have been Teasdale's major symbols of creativity: the wind as the carrier of "the night-wind murmurs of the sea" with its sense of the deep inner drives of life, which relentlessly compel her even as they have overwhelmed her; and the bird, the image of the singer, able both to soar with the wind and to reflect the ordinary domestic life of a woman in her home. If she were like the tree, then she would be able to combine these three in her life—the elemental life force, the soaring spirit to catch the song, and the self to observe that sense of the world she calls beauty and transmute it into poetry.

Chapter Seven
In Somber Pride

The balance Teasdale sought in her life was increasingly difficult to achieve during the next five years, yet even as it failed her in life, she captured in her poems those moments of exquisite poise which, as she said of the sea, "burn, like stretched silver of a wave, / Not breaking, but about to break." During this period she produced poetry of somber radiance on a scale that she had never before achieved. In her personal life she became increasingly withdrawn; her marriage—a reality for only the limited periods they were actually together—was an illusion that they tried to keep alive in letters that became increasingly querulous and could not hide the growing rifts between them. It was a period of financial insecurity, when Filsinger was seriously concerned with his position with the Lawrence Company, and both were upset about the fact that their expenses continually outpaced their income.

During these years she experienced the death of both parents and her older brother, and the problems of friends intruded on her. Illness, lassitude, depression constantly interfered with sustained poetry writing, with long blank spaces of months without a single lyric to record in her notebook. Yet what she wrote approached greatness—a more clear-eyed view of the human condition and of her own inability to escape it. They are poems of middle age, not the love poems usually associated with the lyric. And they are poems that face life forthrightly, rarely falling into the trap of playing victim, or revealing self-pitying vulnerability. The ambition and rebellious spirit that had propelled her thus far found expression now in a kind of defiance of the defeat of death through the will, the pride and the courage to meet the inescapable end without cowardice. Her poems, often described as displaying resignation because of her stoical acceptance, in fact, avoid the passivity that that word suggests, retaining a vitality even in their fascination with death. And the rhythmic freedom that she had been developing moved her "songs" from their charming tunefulness to a level of music that touched deeper chords.

There were a few brief interludes when Teasdale and her husband were able to enjoy being together—a week's vacation in Lenox, Massachusetts, in January 1921 and a two-week stay near Wheelock's parents in Easthampton that summer, but on the trip to England together in 1923 they were frequently separated by the demands of Filsinger's business. But for the most part their lives moved in different directions. Heavily burdened by the demands of his job, Filsinger added other activities to increase his income and his prestige as an expert in international trade. At Teasdale's insistent urgings, he took a few vacations without her—a camping trip on one occasion and a visit to Yellowstone on another—while she continued her practice of taking long retreats from the city to Boonton, New Jersey, or to Concord, Massachusetts, among other places, usually in the spring and, when her spirits were exceptionally low, back to the sanitarium at Cromwell. In 1924 she traveled to Europe for about two months without him and he went to Cuba, Europe, and Egypt in 1925 without her. Even when they were together in the city, their paths diverged. Because her energies were at a low ebb, Teasdale rarely accepted social engagements, sending her husband off without her. For much of the time during the trip they took together to Europe, Filsinger was engaged in handling his business affairs while his wife waited for him in London. The tone of the letters they exchanged continued to contain the affectionate openings and closings, but they were now more superficial decoration to a substratum of petty arguments and sarcasms.

The numerous friends and the literary gossip of New York no longer seemed to interest Teasdale. She avoided the meetings of the Poetry Society, even arranging a trip in order not to attend the annual dinner at which she was to be a guest of honor.[1] When her name was proposed for membership on the executive committee, she declined, claiming ill health. Her letters reveal her growing disillusion with the poets she knew. To her husband she complained of "Frost's ill-temper under criticism . . . and his fulsome and evidently so false praise of Louis' [Untermeyer] poems—the most *terribly* overdone thing I ever saw," and of the "quarrelsome conceit" of Edgar Lee Masters.[2] An advantage to being out of New York, she wrote John Fletcher, was being "a stranger to the politics of literary cliques. I know too much of the inside of things here."[3]

She did not, however, cut herself off completely, writing long letters and using the telephone as her mode of communication with her close friend Marguerite Wilkinson. Their conversations were a vital link, so much a part of the daily routine that they were nick-named "the Teasdaily-Wilkinsonian." John Wheelock continued to be a dependable friend, visiting her even when her husband was away and serving as her escort. One friend whose troubled life did interrupt Teasdale's retreat was Vachel Lindsay. After her decision not to marry him in 1915, he had avoided all contact until 1917, when he felt they might be able to meet with equanimity. At that time, the Filsingers gave a party in his honor, and the friendship, this time including her husband, was resumed. When his book *The Golden Book of Springfield,* published in 1920, failed to receive either critical or popular approval, he wrote to Teasdale for advice. Her attitude toward him seems to have been extremely maternal and he came to rely on her encouragement and support. His emotional control, limited at best, failed him almost completely after the death of his mother in 1922, and more and more often he wrote to Teasdale letters of anguish, culminating in a flood of long rambling letters in 1924 that clearly disturbed her. She stemmed the tide somewhat by informing him that she was taking a rest cure and could neither receive nor send letters, and was delighted to learn some months later that he had married. Lindsay had written one of his most beautiful poems, "The Chinese Nightingale," to Teasdale, so her wedding gift of a white Chinese shawl may have been a symbolic way of passsing to his wife the supportive role she had played.

Rainbow Gold

The success of her anthology of women's poetry in 1917 encour-aged her to do another collection as a way to earn additional money, this time poems intended for children between the ages of ten and fourteen. Entitled *Rainbow Gold,* it became one of her most successful ventures. Showing extraordinary insight into young people's taste, she ruled out all poems written for children, and all moralistic work. Earlier she had written, "Children, who are all really barbarians, should be given the sort of poetry that semi-barbarous people make and enjoy—ballads full of primitive and even brutal feeling. If this were done, there would be joy and not disgust whenever a poem appears on the page of a school reader."[4] She chose standard English classics plus a few modern works, including "La Belle Dame Sans Merci" by Keats, even though one friend counseled against it, feeling that virtuous parents might object.[5] There is more than a little blood and thunder; verses about heroic figures and leprechauns mix with poems about death and love; ancient ballads and contemporary narratives are placed next to songs and lyrics.

By opening with Coleridge's "Kubla Khan," Teasdale set a tone of the wonder and mystery of the imagination that continued throughout the volume. A suggestion of the passing seasons is made by the order, with poems of spring at the beginning and winter poems at the end. The bulk of the poems come from the nineteenth century with the Romantics, Shelley, Keats, Byron, and Wordsworth prominently represented, but a full range of the work of the century is given from Scott to Browning to Swinburne. Lyrics by Shakespeare, Milton, Ben Jonson, Christopher Marlowe, and Robert Herrick represent the early masters. The poets are primarily English, but Americans such as Poe, Longfellow, Emerson and Whitman are also included. Although most of the poets are men, the work of a few women—Emily Dickinson, Julia Ward Howe, Anna Hempstead Branch, and, of course, Christina Rossetti—appears also. The feature that unified the collection, above all, Teasdale pointed out in her preface: She wanted to include

what I and my friends had enjoyed as children, particularly poems with highly accented rhythms. They enjoyed certain sad poems as much as merry ones, but meditative, moralistic and gloomy poems were never read but once, if they were read at all. And I am glad to say that poems full of sentimentality fared no better.[6]

Her selection seems to mirror the taste that T. S. Eliot spoke of when recalling his own first experience with reading poetry.

That the book did in fact appeal to children is underscored by the review in *Poetry* written by Eunice Tietjen's young daughter who said that she was put off when she saw it included "Oh Captain, My Captain," but that when she began to read "I didn't put it down till I had read every printed word between the covers. Even now that I know it so well, I try not to look up anything in it unless I have plenty of time, because I know that I shall sit down and begin it all over again."[7] As Drake commented, "The collection is still a classic of its kind, although changing taste and the difficulty young people now find in reading complex poetic language and earlier forms of English have rendered it less accessible than it was when published."[8] During her work on the anthology, Teasdale's father died and, grief stricken, she threw herself more completely into the project, which she dedicated "to the Beautiful Memory of My Father, John Warren Teasdale." A brief unfinished quatrain is recorded in her notebooks to mark his death; it begins "He loved all lovely things . . ." and she confessed her sense of loss only months later to her sister-in-law. "I think of him so very, very often, and dream of him far too often for my own good—but I don't seem able to break off."[9]

Reading and Approach to Poetry

Part of her increasing solitude was devoted to a more stringent program of reading. In addition to her regular custom of reading all the important new volumes of poetry and the works of her friends such as H. D., Millay, Wylie, Robinson, Houseman, and Masefield, she added serious prose such as Darwin's *The Origin of Species* and Hendrik Van Loon's *The Story of Mankind*, several novels by Stendhal, Dumas fils and Balzac in French, and Melville's *Moby-Dick*. She reread Shakespeare's history plays, and Chekhov, Ibsen, and Gorky were included as was a fourth reading of Yeats's *Wild Swans at Coole*. A surprising entry is *The Dead City* by D'Annunzio, a favorite from her Potter days, read now perhaps because of the death of Eleonora Duse in Pittsburgh in 1924. Milton's *Samson Agonistes* and Tolstoy's *Kreutzer Sonata* must have accentuated her somber mood. The most significant readings were, however, her study of Joyce, Pound, and Eliot. She had read *Portrait of the Artist* just before the publication of *Flame and Shadow*, but during this period she went through all Joyce's then-published works, including *Ulysses*, *Chamber Music*, *Exiles*, and *Dubliners*, as well as a study of Joyce by Herbert Gorman. Her reaction to his writing at least as she wrote about it to her husband was predictable: she admired his psychological insight, but was dismayed by his too-open revelations.[10] Eliot fared less well in her estimation. Writing to Untermeyer, she agreed with his early estimation of *The Waste Land* as a "pompous parade of erudition" and made mention of several of its other faults.[11]

Teasdale's ideas about her poetry did not change substantially from those she had developed while working on the poems included in *Flame and Shadow*, although certain new features were emphasized when she wrote, in response to a series of questions sent by a Professor

Lewis, what she called "The Pattern of a Poem." She attributed it specifically to her subconscious mind and focused more on the rhythm of a poem than on its melody:

> The patterns of most of my lyrics are a matter of balance and speed rather than a matter of design which can be perceived by the eye. The pattern of "The Unchanging" in *Flame and Shadow* is necessarily very simple for the poem is only eight lines long. It consists of the balancing of a picture of the sea shore against the mood of the maker of the poem. The poem rises swiftly for the first three lines and subsides on the slower fourth line. It rises again for two lines and subsides finally on the slow last two lines. The short and very slow last line is an emotional echo of the fourth line. [12]

This change in focus reflects her abandonment of strict metrics in creating her verse, which could be seen in a number of poems in the earlier book, but which was to become more prominent in the new one. She underscored this change in her note to Professor Lewis by saying, "the best modern poets cannot be pinned down to regular and exact meters for very long." The concern with pleasing her audience, which had led to many of the mawkish poems included in *Love Songs* had also been abandoned as she confessed, "Often I am seeking not so much communication with my reader as a better understanding of myself." [13]

Dark of the Moon

During this period there were long spells during which Teasdale could produce no poems worth including in her notebooks. And even those she carefully copied show signs of much more vigorous, ruthless rewriting after having reached that previously regarded "finished" state. When she finally decided to assemble a group of poems for publication, she was equally ruthless in her decisions about which ones to include and which to omit, leaving out many poems that should not be ignored and that Drake has included in his new collection. Such a careful pruning produced a collection of extraordinarily high quality in which the relationship of humanity to the world of nature is explored with great subtlety. While the volume has frequently been regarded as the work of a woman "in love with death," it is also the work of a poet who regards memory as the source of poetry and sees the combination of memory and poetry providing the beauty that is the bulwark against death.

The fifty-nine poems in *Dark of the Moon* were grouped into nine sections so carefully ordered that Teasdale would write Filsinger that "every poem has a reason for being where it is."[14] As with her previous volume in which the sections reflected the polarities of the title, the sections in this book play on varying sorts of opposition of moonlight and darkness. The darkness here is both the darkness of night and the darkness of death, as unknown a territory as the dark side of the moon. The sections alternate between the world of nature and the world of humanity, and in each case she is intent on portraying both the light that comes from the dark and the dark that comes from light.

Section 1, "There Will Be Stars," points up one feature desired by all astronomers that is heightened by a darkened moon—the greater visibility of the stars. The first poem is essentially an affirmation of life, inspired by the poet's ability to record the glories of the world in which she lives. The spaciousness of the daylight scene in "On the Sussex Downs"—the downs themselves, the birds flying, the glittering sea, and the presence of a friend—is painted in beautiful colors, yet is specifically denied in the poem as the cause of her joy:

> It was not you, though you were near,
> Though you were good to hear and see,
> It was not earth, it was not heaven
> It was myself that sang in me.
>
> (*MH*, 98–99)

Yet these physical details are the ingredients of the poet's song. However beautiful the world might be, however glad she might be to be with her companion, without the element of song to celebrate them, their value would be lost. In the next poem, "August Night," the long, sweeping lines, regularized by the five stresses per line rather than by any syllable count, capture the sensuousness of night with its "dew-dripping cedars" and "the honey of fragrance." It is the very fact of the darkness that permits the poet and her companion to see the "star-white" light of the glow-worm. The friend, probably Wheelock, who said he recalled the scene,[15] quotes a line from Dante about love and stars, and the communion between the two is felt rather than spoken. The sensuousness is carried over in the next poem along with its focus on the stars, in which the poet imagines the minds of her lover and herself as flying "on wild clouds of thought, naked together." The physicality of the image emphasizes human passion even while denying it. Here, as she was to do in each section, Teasdale modifies the meaning of the opening poem. Just as the lovers in this poem can know only intellectual passion, so in the next three poems other limitations, other kinds of darkness where light has been expected, are stressed. In "Words for an Old Air" love, or at least an unfulfilled love, is a barrier to beauty rather than the medium of its appreciation.

In "Mountain Water" the experience of youthful ecstasy makes all later experience pall in comparison. In "At Tintagil" the joy of love is almost, but not quite, overwhelmed by the sorrow of its loss. The elements listed in the opening poem, "Earth, Heaven and Lover," reappear in the concluding one, now seen at night, more particularized than in the early one. The affirmation of the first poem is restated in a new form. "There Will Be Stars" is one of Teasdale's best-known poems, written in November 1923 and published first in the *Yale Review* in January 1925. The notebook shows the extensive revision that Teasdale gave it. The original version is as follows:

> There will be stars over the place forever,
> After the house and the street we love are gone
> After the city itself is fallen, forsaken,
> Stars will come with the sunset and go with the dawn.
>
> There will be pasture land where the city clamored,
> And only a waste after mankind is lost—
> But every time the earth circles her orbit
> On the night the autumn equinox is crossed
>
> Two stars we knew, poised on the peak of midnight
> Will reach their zenith; where the sky is steep—
> There will be stars over the place forever
> There will be stars forever while we sleep.
>
> (Poetry Notebook)

Here is the final version:

> There will be stars over the place forever,
> Though the house we loved and the street we loved are lost,

> Every time the earth circles her orbit
>   On the night the autumn equinox is crossed
> Two stars we knew, poised on the peak of midnight
>   Will reach their zenith; stillness will be deep;
> There will be stars over the place forever,
>   There will be stars forever, while we sleep.
>
> *(MH, 100)*

By omitting the four lines describing the destruction of the world
Teasdale accomplished a number of objectives. The focus of the
poem is now concretized by its focus on individuals rather than the
mass of people. The "we" who share a love for a particular house
and street seem to merge into the "two stars," suggesting lovers
whose attachment to each other is so great that they need to imagine
their existence together even after death. The lines about the destruction of the city and of mankind had introduced elements far
too vast to be sustained by the particular imagery employed here
while distracting the reader's attention from the lovers who see the
correspondence between themselves and the stars.

The word changes in the poem provide an insight into Teasdale's
remarkable sense of the rhythms of lyric poetry. In line 2, the
substitution of "though" for "after" destroys the possibility of a
heavily accented rhythm that might be read in too sing-song a
manner. By changing "gone" to "lost" she retained the low, almost
moaning quality of the *o* sounds, but moved the idea out of all sense
of purposeful action into a feeling of the vagaries of fate. The change
in the sixth line from "where the sky is deep" to "stillness will be
deep" illustrates the way a prosaic expression becomes a musical
one. But it is the repetition of "we loved" after "the house" as well
as after "the street" that gives the poem a chantlike quality, even
as it destroys the regularity of the meter. Enhanced by the other
repetitions, it produces the effect of a primitive seer who controls
the world of nature through the power of words. The stars *will* be
there, the reader feels, because the poet's song has the ability to
make them return. The elements announced in the opening poem,
"On Sussex Downs"—earth, heaven, lover, there seen as separate
qualities—have joined together in the harmony of the heavens. Yet
the poem avoids sentimentality or easy optimism in its awareness
of the inevitable destruction of earthly things. The harmony, the

immortality, does exist, the poet says, but there is no foolish pretense that the world can escape disintegration.

The second section contrasts with the first by emphasizing the shadowiness of the human world seen in the dim, autumnal light and the paradoxical quality of the book's title finds a new expression. "Pictures of Autumn" contains just four poems that grew out of the trip to Europe Teasdale had taken with her cousin in 1924, and though the quantity is small, the poems convey a depth of feeling that puts them far ahead of the earlier travel poems included in *Rivers,* where the particular place described is used only to evoke an emotion, and the concentration on perfect metrical form occasionally seems cloying. The opening "Autumn (Parc Monceau)" is particularly free in its line lengths and stresses, yet the rhythms never seem awkward, stabilized by the recurring three-stress lines. The opening line, "I shall remember. . . ," introduces a quality that permeates the poem; the scene and the poet's observation of it exist, not for the moment itself, but for the memory of it, the memory that the poem itself makes permanent. The autumnal mood appeals to the senses with the colors and the water foreshadowing the sensuousness of the statue of Venus, whose arms ambiguously both hide and accentuate her breasts. The reflection of the colonnade in the pool is disturbed by the leaves floating on the surface so that it "seems lost in the mass of leaves and unavailing / As a dream lost among dreams" (*MH,* 104). The image of a particular dream being confused and distorted by other, more recent dreams reflects back on the opening words, "I shall remember." Despite the poet's insistence that she will hold this scene in her mind forever, she is aware that in fact she will forget it, that the events of her life will crowd it out and that it, too, will become "a dream lost among dreams." Thus the poem is the only remembrance, made more poignant by its realization of the frailty of the human mind.

In "September Day (Pont de Neuilly)" Teasdale describes the Seine river flowing through Paris "out of the mist and into the mist again" with the autumn leaves drifting out to sea. While the poem seems a simple description, the line "Nothing remembers or grieves" forces a comparison to human responses. People *do* remember and they *will* grieve at the loss and death that the trees, leaves, and river accept patiently. It is this ability that distinguishes humans from other earthly things, but it is also a quality that brings human misery.

Memory as history informs the next poem, "Fontainebleau," a place Teasdale described on a postcard as "like an Amy Lowell poem."[16] Here the poet re-creates the world when the palace was new. The poem records the movement from the interior of the palace with its "ladies lovely and immoral" into the garden, where "the crimson and scarlet and rose-red dahlias" mimic the women's makeup. But the gardens are "desolately gay," the bleak melancholy quality of the adjective undercutting the beauty of the scene. As the poem moves from the garden into the surrounding forest, the "desolate" quality is replaced by the more ominous sounds of the hunters chasing a boar, the dark tones of violence and blood reflecting back on the sensuousness of the earlier stanzas. The romanticized images of kings and knights and ladies in ancient palaces that had been so much a part of Teasdale's earlier poetry are now reseen in more realistic terms with a sense of the not-always-attractive force of human passions. Yet the poem ends by returning the scene to the past, back to the romantic illusions: "But the sound of horse and horn are hushed in falling leaves, / Four centuries of autumns, four centuries of leaves" (MH, 104). The difference now is that the poet has both shown us the scene and has let us know that its fine romantic illusion serves the useful purpose of hiding the evils of the past.

The paradoxical nature of darkness and light is expressed in the third section, "Sand Drift," with its focus on the sea. From it Teasdale derives a sense of the eternity of the sea, yet it is also a force that will eradicate all traces of human life. The sea figures in each of the poems—as some joyful giant in the first, "Beautiful, Proud Sea"; as a sterile passion in the second, "Lands End"; as a harsh, unchanging, destructive force in the third, "Sand Drift." Human efforts to recapture past experiences in "Blue Stargrass" are doomed to failure. The threatening "blackness of the sea" coexists with the suggested passion of the red star in "September Night," and in the final poem, "Low Tide," the eternity of the sea seems to mock the end of the year and its reminder of human death.

With the fourth section the focus returns to humanity and the paradox of the volume's title finds expression in the paradox of life: that it is possible to learn from experience, but the value of that knowledge or the expression of it in words may be less than useful. The opening poem, "Effigy of a Nun (Sixteenth Century)," was written when Teasdale and Jean Starr Untermeyer went together in the spring of 1921 to the Cloisters in upper Manhattan and both wrote poems about the tomb. Untermeyer's poem recalls the event itself:

A Dead Nun Smiles at Two Poets

The sun was smiling lazy smiles
   And crinkling all the winter weather;
He planted spring for miles and miles
   And drew two women friends together.

Each sauntered from her separate hill
   And, when they met, walked by the river
Discussing modern love until
   Their pliant hearts began to quiver.

Now Art impinges on our lives
   And complicates our strange position;
We balk at being maids or wives,
   Intolerant of all tradition.
       ****
The sun with manly mischief beamed
   Upon each brow till it grew moister;
He meant to force these two, it seemed,
   Into a cool adjacent cloister.

And through a crack in its dim room
   He touched a spot with shining finger
Where, smiling even on her tomb,
   A sleeping lady made them linger.

With hands that clasped a rigid cross,
   She who foreswore both Art and Eros,
Now dryly seemed to mourn the loss
   Of what had made her life a hero's. [17]

Untermeyer had obviously taken the opportunity to produce a little joke, but Teasdale used the occasion to produce a more profound analysis of the dead woman, eventually published in *Bookman*. In contrast to the Portuguese nun in *Helen of Troy* for whom she imagined a moment of divine forgiveness for the sin of passion, Teasdale here paints a portrait of a woman who knows all too well the price she has paid in choosing the cloistered life, who has kept her vows even though she has suffered through the loneliness they brought. A proud woman, she kept her own counsel and viewed her world with detached amusement, regarding the lack of love as great as having it. In the concluding stanzas Teasdale suggests the thoughts she imagines the woman having:

> She who so loved herself and her own warring thoughts,
>   Watching their humorous, tragic rebound,
> In her thick habit's fold, sleeping, sleeping,
>   Is she amused by dreams she has found?
>
> Infinite tenderness, infinite irony,
>   Are hidden forever in her closed eyes,
> Who must have learned too well in her long loneliness
>   How empty wisdom is, even to the wise.
>
>   (*MH*, 86)

The poem reflects much of what Teasdale's own life must have seemed to her to have been at that time—a choice made for a marriage that now seemed to lack love, the pride in keeping a vow even though it doomed her to loneliness, and, above all, calm and the refusal to talk about it in public.

The last poem, "So This Was All," sums up the meaning of the section and carries it to new heights. The poem was not included in the collected poems that Teasdale arranged before her death, perhaps because its theme of life as a play seemed to her trite or because the message seemed too pessimistic, but it is one of her more extraordinary achievements and has been included in Drake's edition. Part of the pleasure comes from the realization that it is an almost perfect sonnet, using the same Italian form she had labored over in her early years. The contrast between those adolescent efforts and this one marks the great maturity as an artist that she had achieved.

> So this was all there was to the great play
>   She came so far to act in, this was all—
> Except the short last scene and the slow fall
> Of the final curtain, that might catch half-way,
> As the final curtains do, and leave the grey
>   Lorn end of things too long exposed. The hall
>   Clapped faintly, and she took her curtain call,
> Knowing how little she had left to say.

> And in the pause before the last act started,
> Slowly unpinning the roses she had worn,
> She reconsidered lines that had been said,
> And found them hardly worthy the high-hearted
> Ardor that she had brought, nor the bright, torn
> Roses that shattered round her, dripping red.
>
> (*MH*, 103)

The three sentences that make up the poem meld the rhythms of natural speech with the poetic form. The careful placement of stressed syllables as in "great play," and "short last scene" and "grey lorn end" lengthen out key terms and slow the lines to accent the ironic or melancholy tone, while the same technique in the closing lines, the "bright, torn" and "dripping red," accentuates the sense of an unhealed wound that deepens the quiet sadness to a more serious level that reflects back on the total poem. As the poem of a middle-aged woman looking back on her life, it produces an ominous note only slightly softened by the half-amused attitude of the narrator. Words, all the words of a lifetime, are given little value, and it is silence containing the knowledge of secret sorrow that has assumed importance.

The central section, "Midsummer Nights," balances the great light of the moon with the smaller lights of the stars, and while the group contains one of the most pessimistic poems, it also includes one of the most optimistic. A careful contrast is made among the poems. The opening two describe, first, moonlight on the East Coast on the sea, "Twilight (Nahant)," and then on the West Coast on the land, "Full Moon (Santa Barbara)"; the next two poems contrast the ocean with a fountain and moonlight with starlight. In both its beginning and its end, the section asserts a belief in some divine force that governs life, but in the central poems all the symbols of eternity that once were reassuring now are foreboding.

The focus on nature is balanced by the human concerns of section 6, this time those of the poetic narrator herself, emphasizing the positive values derived from the darkness of loneliness. Avoiding any sense of resignation or wistful melancholy, the title poem, "The Crystal Gazer," presents a narrator, aloof from humanity, watching "the little shifting pictures of people rushing / In restless self-importance to and fro." The poem emphasizes the narrator's strength of will in being able to "take my scattered selves and make them

one," a process that gives her the vision and detachment to watch
the rest of humanity with patronizing contempt. The strength of
this self-containment is reasserted in the next poem, "The Solitary."
Enriched by her life experiences, she no longer needs people and
has less need to "shape my thoughts into words." Unconcerned with
others, she relies on her own powers:

> Let them think I love them more than I do,
>   Let them think I care, though I go alone;
> If it lifts their pride, what is it to me
>   Who am self-complete as a flower or a stone.
>   (*CP,* 179)

The sense of self-reliance in "Day's Ending (Tucson)" recalls the
time when Teasdale visited Marion Cummings Stanley in Arizona,
some thirteen years earlier, trying to overcome the intense pain of
neurasthenia from which she was suffering. In "A Reply" she is
almost contemptuous in her rejection of human sympathy: "So waste
no sympathy on me / Or any well-meant gallantry." Having had
four people who she felt knew her, she is content. Not only does
she reject the overtures of others, but in "Leisure" she now feels no
need to communicate: "Sharing with no one but myself the frosty /
And half ironic musings of my mind." The ultimate aloneness of
death has become attractive and in "I Shall Live to Be Old" she
questions the value of long life, but she returns to the value of
memory in life, shrewdly observing in "Wisdom" that "what we
have never had, remains; / It is the things we have that go." Memories are the great compensation she finds in the loneliness of her
middle years, and if intense desire and passion have gone, their
passing has also lessened the fear she felt at death; it is yet another
value found in the absence of fire and light, another light from the
"Dark of the Moon." Yet it has its own darkness, for it signals an
end to her songs, in "The Old Enemy":

> Rebellion against death, the old rebellion
>   Is over; I have nothing left to fight;
> Battles have always had their meed of music
>   But peace is quiet as a windless night.
>
> Therefore I make no songs—I have grown certain
>   Save when he comes too late, death is a friend,

> A shepherd leading home his flock serenely
> Under the planet at the evening's end.
>
> (*MH*, 94)

It should be noted, however, that she was able to write a poem about not writing poems, struggling as always to produce the precise effect she wanted, as the notebook entries show. Originally she had written only about one "battle" and had said the rebellion "has left me." The new version sharpens the metaphor. Line 6 was the one that caused the most trouble, with three versions attempted: "Death is a friend save when he comes too late"; and "That death is gentle, coming as a friend," were the rejected versions. The acceptance of death that this poem enunciates is so calmly made, it seems to reject any self-pitying attitude toward the frustrations of life, looking at the cycle of life in an unflinching manner and finding the good in it.

"Berkshire Notes," section 7, moves back to the natural world, finding a brightness in winter where she had usually seen only bleakness and barrenness. The first four poems and the title commemorate the happy week she and her husband enjoyed in 1923, while the final poems question the value of spring, which had been for her a season of hope, ending with the brief quatrain "Autumn Dusk" which returns to rewards of a solitary existence.

> I saw above a sea of hills
> A solitary planet shine,
> And there was no one near or far
> To keep the world from being mine.
>
> (*MH*, 89)

The merger of the solitary planet and the narrator, like the melding of the two stars in "There Will Be Stars," suggests a communion achieved that is greater than the communion of people, a communion possible specifically because of the absence of people.

This self-sufficiency dominates section 8, as the poems move back to a focus on the human, and even the possible communion with the stars is denied in the opening poem, "Arcturus in Autumn," which is also the title for the sequence. Teasdale later said this was one of her favorite poems. It draws on her knowledge of astronomy, to point out that this star first appears in the northern hemisphere in spring and disappears in autumn. Extraordinary musicality of lines like "There in the thickening dark a wind-bent tree above me / Loosed its last leaves in flight," the slowness of phrases like "thickening dark" and "wind-bent tree" contrast with the almost whispering alliteration at the end, captured in "Restless as dwindling streams that still remember / The music of their flood." The star moving on its predestined course without pity for human plight abandons humanity in its darkest hours.

The ability the poet claims for herself in "I Could Snatch a Day" to reverse the seasons or "to take the heavy wheel of the world and break it," lies idle as she sits "brooding while the ashes fall / cowering over an old fire that dwindles, / waiting for nothing at all." She echoes the despair, as Drake has pointed out, more commonly associated with the modern poets she had rejected, such as T. S. Eliot.[18] The rest of the poems in the group, however, reject that despair and return to the self-sufficiency, the pride, and the will to shape her life. In "An End" she assumes control, even though the control can produce nothing but renunciation: "With my own will I vanquished my own heart . . . / With my own will I turned the summer from me. . . ." Communication with people is seen as dangerous in "Foreknown," where the people who bring her some special news are hoping to see her pain, but find her "light as the dry leaves. . . ." "Winter" with its "lessening days" compensates with the "glittering glassy plume on every tree" following the sleet storms. Instead of stars and communion, she will "find at night a friendly ember, / And make my life of what I can remember." Even if her lover comes back, she will not even open the window, in "Winter Night Song," preferring to "sit by the fire reading. . . ." The rejection is complete in "Never Again," one of the few poems in which even the grammatical structure of the sentence completely breaks down, mirroring the confusion of her own mind as she rejects the restorative powers of song: "Never again the melody that lightly / Caressed my grief and healed the wounds it gave." The exquisite lines of the last poem of the group, "The Tune," recalls "A Minuet of Mozart's" in *Helen of Troy*. Although the earlier poem had caught the same sense of melody reaching to the heights, it lacked the direct connection to life presented here and the skyrocket descent that so poignantly captures the pointlessness of death. The poem escapes sentimentality or self-pity by the total detachment of the poet, by the sense that a level of beauty had been achieved.

The final section, "The Flight," has the same stoic acceptance, finding light in the darkness of failed human relationships. In "The Beloved" the poet accepts the limited closeness with her beloved, honored for having known him better than the rest have known. Yet loneliness without the lover is intolerable in "When I Am Not with You," where even her "poor pride bows down." "Dedication," heavily reworked in the notebook, achieves extraordinary tightness through the revisions particularly apparent in the third stanza:

In the first version it reads:

> Let it live on your lips like a song,
> Let it fly like a flag unfurled
> Let it fold like a cloak around you
> Against the wind of the world.
> (Poetry Notebook)

In the second version:

> Let it live on your lips like a song
> Let it be to your hunger, bread
> Let it be to your weariness, sleep
> And the pillow under your head.
> (Poetry Notebook)

And in the final version:

> Let my love be the pillow
> Under your head,
> On your lips like a song,
> To your hunger, bread.
> (*Dark of the Moon,* 89)

Economy, rather than musicality, seems the new standard, a harmony built on cadence rather than melody. The chantlike quality of the repeated "Let" of the original seems pretentious compared with the simplicity of the revised version.

Pride reasserts itself in "On a March Day," which asks her companion to "bear witness for me that I loved my life, / All things that hurt me and all things that healed. . . ." And to that defiant oath she adds, "I ceased to fear, as once I feared, / The last complete reunion with the earth." The presence of the companion is a vital

factor, and of that companion the poet asks in the next poem, "Let
it be you who shut my eyelids . . . / With the old look, with the
old whisper, and without tears." And it is of that companionship
the final poem speaks

The Flight

We are two eagles
Flying together
Under the heavens
Over the mountains,
Stretched on the wind.
Sunlight heartens us,
Blind snow baffles us,
Clouds wheel after us
Ravelled and thinned.

We are like eagles,
But when Death harries us,
Human and humbled
When one of us goes,
Let the other follow,
Let the flight be ended,
Let the fire blacken,
Let the book close.

                                        (*MH*, 96)

It may have been the tight organizational scheme that she had
created for *Dark of the Moon* that caused Teasdale to omit from the
volume so many excellent poems. It was not reticence, for most of
the poems had appeared in magazines over the years, although she
may have felt that limited exposure was sufficient revelation. It may
be that the bleakness of the thought of the omitted poems would
overwhelm the volume, destroyed the balance she had tried to achieve,
however shakily, between poems of brightness and darkness. For
the most part, the poems that were omitted chronicle the battles
that raged within her.

Many of these poems enunciate with clarity the problems faced
by women who have accepted conventional standards of behavior,
but often they deal with the problems common in all human attempts at communication. A group of poems provides an insight
into the cost of being with people, reflecting the message Teasdale

had written in a letter to Amy Lowell, complimenting her on a new volume of poetry, finding her "more violent and delicate" than she had suspected. She said that she longed to talk with her, but then added, even if they did have the chance to talk,

I'd find myself putting up the veil on one side and tacking it neatly, while you, on your side, were hammering at a nail to keep it secure at the other end. And we'd talk of editors and publishers and the latest English poet to come over—just as we usually do. And my mind, which is a neat little machine, would keep itself pleasantly concealed, while you were cutting yours down so as to fit the apparent size of mine—and there we'd be. Well, there's no use. [19]

The need to conceal one's feelings in society informs "It Is Not I," a poem that describes the polite, self-deprecating attitude of the poet when she is with other people, encouraging them to talk about themselves while she conceals her own concerns. The poet exists only for an unnamed person: "It is not I they love, there is no I / Except for you who have me for your own."

The reason for hiding herself from people is given in "Armor," where she talks of her pride like the "shirts of mail . . . forged with such care . . . none knew that it was there." It prevents serious injury, even though the flesh might bleed. The image of armor, as Terence Diggory has pointed out, [20] appears in Emily Dickinson, Elinor Wylie, and several other women poets as a source of protection against too naked a revelation of the self. In the same way, the self is hidden in "A Man Who Understood Women," where, with unconcealed irony, the poet describes a man who thinks he is a lady-killer, while the woman to whom he is talking masks her own amused reactions. Only in "At a Party," in which the poet and her lover are "beautifully, terribly" aware of each other, is a social scene endowed with any positive pleasure, and there the communication exists in spite of the roar of the conversation.

More frequently these poems talk of pain. There is the pain of unfulfilled passion, as in "Ashes to Ashes," where the suffering narrator tersely tells herself not to worry, "in the course of things it will soon be over now," and in "Absence," where it is described as "secret scourgings of all earth's children," and even the coming of spring in "March Nights" is no longer desirable. Passion wars against her "spartan nature" in "Conflict" and in "Overheard." There is the pain of the inability to satisfy others in "Sleepless Nights" and in the melancholy realization in "After Midnight, London" of the insignificance of the individual. And there is the confusion and frustration and a sense of entrapment in "In the Web," where even the stars are "caught in the trap of space that has no end." Shadows are visualized as chains in "Shadows," yet without them the narrator and her companion wander like wraiths. There is fear of "the stealthy seeker" in "Hide and Seek" and the miasma of fantasy in "I Lived My Life as a Dream" where the failure of memory destroys the links to reality. Above all, there is the fear of death that cannot be conquered even by elaborate enbalming of "Egyptian Kings" and it circles above in "The Hawk," swooping down while passion and reason struggle within the individual. The deterioration of old age is chronicled with grim specificity as the poet watches in "This Hand" "the skin slacken and wrinkle and shine, / The comely shape and color gone." She might, as she suggests in "Autumn Song," avoid thinking about it, just as she avoids picking the thorn-branched holly, but it is only an evasion, not a solution.

The possible escapes are few. She might, as in "The Hour," choose to believe that there is a supernatural power that orders human life, ordaining her meeting with her lover, but she does so "without sorrow and without elation." Or she may retreat from emotion, and become "cool as the touch of stone" in the poem of that name. But such an action means the end of her poetry: "Let your harp stand untouched / With all its slackened wires." Silence assumes a positive value, becoming as much a form of communication as speech itself; like a stone, it is still, but just as a stone has been formed in fire, so her silence has been formed by passion.

Death has been a frequent topic for poetry throughout the ages, and Teasdale's consideration of it places her within an accepted tradition. Rossetti's "Song" has already been compared with Teasdale's "I Shall Not Care," and Emily Brontë's "Remembrance," Tennyson's in "Crossing the Bar" and "Come Not When I Am Dead"; Stevenson's "Requiem" are all just a few of the poems she was familiar with. What makes Teasdale's poems of death in this period unique is perhaps the coolness with which she faces the prospect. In some poems this unflinching response is based on a correspondence she imagines between herself and the stars, as in "There Will Be Stars" or with the flowing of the river in "September Day (Pont de Neuilly)." Sometimes it is the ability to go on dreaming in death, as in "Effigy of a Nun." Or it may be never losing the illusion that one matters, as in "Epitaph." More often, it was the disillusionment with life that made death seem an acceptable alternative, for the rest it provides, as in "Not by the Sea" or "I Shall Live to Be Old." Death is a peaceful return in "The Old Enemy" or an acceptable end in "On a March Day." She assumes that she will be aware of what is happening, as in "Let it be You," or that there is a divine force, the "Friend" in "Midsummer Night" or the "Secret Will" in "Twilight (Nahant)."

But it is the ability within a particular poem to capture the qualities of death and life in a moment of balance that elevates her poems above the level of morbidity. It can best be seen in "The Tune," where she describes her life as a song and goes on to say:

> It climbs and climbs; I watch it sway in climbing
> High over time, high even over doubt,
> It has all heaven to itself—it pauses
> And faltering blindly down the air, goes out.
>
> (*MH, 99*)

As important as the poems of death are the poems about memory. In these poems she seems to be moving away from poetry of experience to poetry based on the memory of the experience. Most of the poems are in the past tense, and even when the present tense is used, as in the sequence "Pictures of Autumn," the scene that is described is captured explicitly to be stored in memory. Memory is even preferable to trying to relive the experience. In "Blue Stargrass" the repeat of a walk to the beach fails because of the many changes:

> Where the sun warmed us
> With a cloak made of gold
> The rain would be falling
> And the wind would be cold.
>
> And we would stop to search
> In the wind and the rain,
> But we would not find the stargrass
> By the path again.
>
> (*MH, 75*)

Conversely, the attempt to repeat the experience will fail because of the sameness, as in "Sand Drift," when she goes again to the dunes:

> Nothing has changed; with the same hollow thunder
> The waves die in their everlasting snow—
> Only the place we sat is drifted over,
> Lost in the blowing sand, long, long ago.
>
> (MH, 94)

Present experience seems to pall in comparison to memory. In "Mountain Water" the memory of the "drink from a wild fountain" guarantees that "the springs that flow on the floor of the valley will never seem fresh or clear." Or present experience is ominous, speaking only of endings. In "Low Tide" she complains "When nothing is left but the old year dying / Why did you bring me down to the sea?" and "In the Wood" the beauty of the scene "Lured me gently, gently, happy and alone, / Suddenly a heavy snake / Reared black upon a stone."

But memory is a bulwark. It is memory that sustains Iseult in "At Tintagil" even though much of it was painful. It fills the poet-narrator's life in "A Reply": "I have enough to do to muse / On memories I would not lose." And she spends her "Leisure" turning over the "frosty and half ironic musings of my mind." It can occupy her in "Winter" when she will "make my life of what I can remember." Yet memory can also be dangerous. In the poem "Water Lilies" published in *American Miscellany* in 1922, the poet says that if you remember the "sight of flowers," try to avoid going back, for "the shadow of the mountain . . . [will fall] on your heart."

But memory in general, regardless of the force of any particular remembrance, provides the point of balance between inner and outer reality. In "I Have Seen the Spring," it is difficult to tell if the poet is describing a current or a remembered scene:

> Nothing is new, I have seen spring too often;
> There have been other plum-trees white as this one
> Like a silvery cloud tethered beside the road,
> I have been waked from sleep too many times
> By birds at dawn boasting their love is beautiful.
> The grass-blades gleam in the wind, nothing is changed.
> Nothing is lost, it is all as it used to be,

Unopened lilacs are still as deep a purple,
The boughs of the elm are dancing still in a veil of tiny leaves,
Nothing is lost but a few years from my life.

(MH, 92)

Through the power of memory, past and present merge in the vision
of the eternal beauties of spring, and the poet's mental picture finds
an exact correspondence in the scene around her. The momentary
nature of the balance is caught in the bitterly ironic conclusion.

Many of these poems tell of the search for some rules, some
meaning to life. This effort, caught with a sense of desperation in
a letter to Rittenhouse, is expressed here as a sense of loss. Constrained by the puritan mores, she lacked the firmness of the faith:

I am borne onward from the faith of my fathers
  It is far behind me, like a fading song,
But sometimes I am homesick for its triumphant certainties,
  I who must break my heart to learn the right from wrong.

(MH, 69)

Occasionally she projected some sense of a Divine will, and those
poems, such as "Nahant" and "Midsummer Night," were included
in *Dark of the Moon*, but many other questioning ones, such as the
one quoted above, were omitted, as if to keep secret this doubting
side of her nature. The relentless way of the world was a "trap of
space that has no end," and the divinity is seen as the "Great Captor"
in "In the Web." Life seems, in "Hide and Seek," like a

Game in the dark,
A groping in shadows, a brief exultance, a dread
Of what may couch beside us or lurk behind us,
A leaving of what we want to say unsaid,
Sure of one thing only, a long sleep
When the game is over and we are put to bed.

(MH, 92)

Without a sustaining faith, the questioning was like a war within
her, characterized as the struggle between the Spartan and the Sybarite in "Conflict" that seems unending, her "slow blood dripping
wet." When the end has come, she realizes, "I shall be the defeated

one." Or it is a war between "two quarrelling shepherds, The Flesh and the Mind" in "The Hawk."

In the face of these struggles, silence seems the best response. Silence, which had begun to assume a significance in a few poems in *Flame and Shadow*, appears now as something more than the absence of sound. Behind the silence lies a secret knowledge that can yield secret power. The silence of the woman in "Effigy of a Nun" is seen as a source of strength, an understanding of life that she knew better than to repeat, and in her death that knowledge is conveyed through the wordless medium of her expression. And silence dominates the poems in section 4 of the book. "Those Who Love" mentions the silence of the great lovers of the past and of a woman who, "fighting in somber pride," never mentioned her unfulfilled love. In "Epitaph," written to commemorate the death of Madison Cawein, who had proposed Teasdale for membership in the Poetry Society, death is described as silent as "a red leaf's descending . . . the unending / Drawing of all things to the earth again." The poet's "So be it . . . ." suggests that this willed acceptance is the better way, since "the earth will not regret her tireless lover, / Nor he awaken to know she does not care." The implication is that if there were some message it would be one that would tell of the insignificance of even a lover of nature in the scheme of the world. "Appraisal" applauds the silence of the woman about her lover's faults and also the inability of language to express his virtues. "The Wise Woman" who can give up a particularly beautiful moment must have some secret store from which she can draw, or she has the secret wisdom, "how much more safe it is to lack / A thing that time so often steals." Silence thus is equated with secret wealth or power, and it is this secret strength that enables the woman in the whimsical "She Who Could Bind You" to hold the lover. Silence is a quality of peacefulness in contrast to the music of battle in "The Old Enemy" and provides the excuse for giving up poetry. Important messages are the ones that come without words, such as the pleasure of a day in the eyes of a lover in "Winter Sun (Lenox)." It is silence in "Wisdom," in which the "shadows and the wind / Listen for what was never spoken" that unmentioned love remains. Had it been mentioned, it, too, would have been like "the things we have that go." And it is the silence in death that will speak most loudly to her beloved as her silence had in life:

You will know then all that in silence
You always knew,
Though I have loved, I loved no other
As I love you.

(*MH,* 101–2)

Images of light had served throughout Teasdale's poetry as signals for passion and for knowledge, but here the burning power of sunlight has been replaced by the moon and stars, which themselves give way to the embers in a dying fire. The silvered tone of moonlight lends a sense of gleaming austerity to the verses. It is the "wintry moon, white as a flower" ("At Tintigal") rather than the flames in earlier poems that shone for Iseult; it is the "high moon, most reticent and queenly" that speaks of the "wisdom of the Law" in "Twilight (Nahant)." The few mentions of the brighter light of the sun or of fire are specifically denied. In "Ashes to Ashes" the poet admonishes herself to "shut your heart, though it be like a burning house." And the brightness she might have chosen in "If I Could Snatch a Day," "sharp blue skies with new leaves shining, / And flying shadows cast by flying wings," is rejected.

But without the bright light of the sun and even the lesser light of the moon, Teasdale, schooled as she was in astronomy, knew that she could see the stars more clearly, and it is starlight that provides the inspiration, the limited sense of immortality, as in "There Will Be Stars." Yet, by their very constancy, the stars remind her of her own mortality, as in "Clear Evening." With their lesser light, however, they reassure her that even though they are small in the "serene bright multitude . . . even the shyest ones, even the faint motes," are part of the "holy night" ("Midsummer Night"). She can imagine that the stars see her even as she watches them ("February Twilight") and make her feel a sense of power ("Autumn Dusk"). But the immutability of their motions, particularly in "Arcturus in Autumn" seems to make them pitiless. Like the other lights she has known, they also fail to provide the certainty for which she was searching.

The balancing of the contradictory values of light is expressed in "Full Moon (Santa Barbara)," the second stanza of which reads:

I saw far off the grey Pacific bearing
A broad white disk of flame,

And on the garden-walk a snail beside me
Tracing in crystal the slow way he came.
(*MH*, 81–82)

Both the distant vastness of the lighted ocean and the close mi-
nuteness of the earthly creature coexist momentarily and provide
values for humanity.

Equally important as light in Teasdale's poems are images of
water. The sea with its eternal passion does in one beautiful poem
retain that power:

Beautiful, Proud Sea

Careless forever, beautiful proud sea,
  You laugh in happy thunder all alone,
You fold upon yourself, you dance your dance
  Impartially on drift-weed, sand or stone.

You make us believe that we can outlive death,
  You make us for an instant, for your sake,
Burn, like stretched silver of a wave,
  Not breaking, but about to break.
(*MH*, 107)

Written in 1925 during her husband's absence in Cuba and Europe,
this poem recaptures the sense of power and passion she had earlier
experienced, but the once optimistic message she had received is
seen in a new light. The poem appears on a quick first reading to
repeat the joyful tone of earlier perceptions—the sea "laughs" and
dances, its music is "happy thunder," the wave is "stretched silver."
More careful attention, however, reveals the extent of self-deception
she now sees in any correspondence to human life. The sight and
sound of the sea "make us believe," that is, cause us to accept a
truth that may only be pretense, the make-believe world of immortality that lasts for only a moment. And that moment is, with
all its pain, the moment of beauty. However much she can still
find the ecstatic in the sea, she is now aware of how much of it is
illusion.

More frequently the sea has become an image of sterility, as in
"Land's End"; of destruction in its blackness, as in "September
Night"; of lack of peace and rest, as in "Not by the Sea." Even the

freedom she once attributed to it is denied in "The Fountain." "It heaves and sags, as the moon runs round; / Ocean and fountain, shadow and tree, / Nothing escapes, nothing is free." She expresses the change in her vision most concretely in "The Sea Lover," where she says:

> I cannot be what the sea is
>   To you who love the sea,
> Its ease of empty spaces,
>   Its soothing majesty;
> To the many moods of the ocean
>   Go back, for here in me
> Is only its sad passion
>   And changeful constancy.
>   (*MH*, 74)

Just as the sea has failed to provide hope, so too the birds and their ability to sing, which had once inspired her, have failed; they have become creatures of darkness and destruction. The happy larks that "sing to the sky" in the opening poem in this book never reappear, their place taken by the gathering birds and the violent fish hawk in "Low Tide," whose "sharp black wings" she envies, and the hawk who swoops to destroy. Instead of singing, there is the "blue jay scolding" in "A December Day"—how different from the blue jay in an earlier poem whose beauty captured the scene for lovers! The flight of birds still has the power to refresh her spirit, captured in the flight in "Two Minds," although its limitations are immediately stated in the scene of the two lovers watching in envy. In "To a Sea Gull in the City" the "lonely and serene delight" of its flight moves her to tears: "The tears that could not fall for my own sorrow, / Have blessed the eyes that lift to watch your flight." She has transmuted the self-pity she feels into compassion for all living creatures. But flight is significant, as witnessed by the final poem in this volume, where the sense of freedom, however glorified, is not without its pain nor is it imagined to be eternal.

The music that had once been attributed to the birds now comes from the wind with harsher tones and destructive force. It is the wind that harries the sea grass endlessly in "Land's End" and blows the sand to destroy the place where she had sat with her lover in "Sand Drift." The sound that was part of the music she connected with the hemlock at the end of her last book continues to provide song but only brings messages of grief in "Wind Elegy (W. E. W.)," written in memory of W. E. Wheeler, or the wind announces the coming of winter in "An End." Only in "On a March Day" does she find a message to support her pride, its dissonance and force matching the defiance of her assertion:

> Here in the teeth of this triumphant wind
>   That shakes the naked shadows on the ground,
> Making a key-board of the earth to strike
>   From clattering tree and hedge a separate sound,
>
> Bear witness for me that I loved my life,
>   All things that hurt me and all things that healed,
> And that I swore to it this day in March,
>   Here at the edge of this new-broken field.
>   (MH, 112)

The wind is frequently portrayed as driving the leaves, and it is the autumn leaves that she identifies with. Leaves represent memories in the poems about Paris or they bring the message of coming winter ("An End"). She identifies herself with the leaves in "I Shall Live to Be Old," clinging "to life as the leaves to the creaking oak" and in "Foreknown" she is "light as dry leaves driven / Before the storm that splits an oak." From those leaves she has learned how to face disillusion: "Lightly, lightly, almost gay, / Taking the unreturning way / To mix with winter and snow."

Despite the fact that Teasdale had omitted many of her darker poems from *Dark of the Moon,* the critics tended to overlook her attempts at a balanced view of life and to note its somber quality. One critic noted "the gleaming austerity"[21] while another described her as a lithe, simple, spontaneous lyricist."[22] Margaret Wilkinson, remarking on the sadness of the lyrics, echoed one of the poems to say "she finds more joy in sorrow than most of us ever find in joy."[23] And the reading public was enthusiastic, buying out the first edition immediately and requiring a second edition within two weeks.

A new note had crept into the critical attitude, however, with some open challenges to traditional poetry that reflected the changing attitudes that had been developing over the years and that found a rallying point with the publication in 1922 of T. S. Eliot's *The Waste Land.* The very features that Teasdale had specifically re-

jected—erudite allusions, surface complexity of thought and structure, dissonance, irregular rhythms—were being treated as positive
values. Genevieve Taggard noted the change when she wrote that the
"present generation wants complexity, rejects delicacy. . . ." She
considered Teasdale "a meager talent with one clear note" although
she was able to point to some poems as worthwhile.[24]

Conrad Aiken, also striving to find new approaches, however,
had looked back to the Elizabethans in an essay on Teasdale published in the *Dial* just the year before.[25] He considered her work
only as "love poetry" and compared it with that of the sixteenth
and seventeenth centuries. Determining that the Elizabethan convention had degenerated by the nineteenth century (even Byron,
Shelley, or Wordsworth were rarely considered first-rate by his standards), he admitted that Teasdale used the convention "pretty com-
petently," but he found that "she pads a great deal . . . her touch
is very unsure. . . . Her sense of metrical fitness is decidedly
intermittent." Aiken's criticism, harking back to standards older
than the current ones, was an attempt to develop an approach that
would foster the more vigorous content in traditional poetry as a
way of countering the work of the more radical elements whose
approach he found equally untenable.

Aiken's essay focused on the earlier, more sentimental poems that
Teasdale produced, talking of "her Strephons and Colins," about
which she had not written for over ten years, although he did concede
that with them, "she comes closest to the Elizabethan manner." It
is a waspish review, pointing more to Aiken's difficulty in finding
an adequate critical approach than to Teasdale's more mature practice. He saw the values in her work, noting her epigrammatical
skill, the charm, but he was making a serious effort, albeit awk-
wardly, to dismiss the overly sentimental verse that had so dominated the poetry scene, and yet not to accept the new approaches
being developed by Pound and Eliot. He was unable to appreciate
that her lack of "metrical fitness" represented a step forward in
adapting traditional poetry to suit the new forms and, more important, he failed to hear the music in her poetry, which is her
highest achievement.

Harriet Monroe, also writing a survey article on Teasdale just a
month after Aiken's, provided a more balanced view, achieved by
viewing Teasdale's work as a development over a period of time,
from the "girlish softness" of the early work to the more austere

and mature work in the later period. She did not refrain from pointing out the limitations, that in giving "the woman's version of the human love-story," it was only "as much of it as one of the finer, more sensitive and protected women of our veiled and walled-in civilization may contribute to the whole vast epic of the race." But she was able to appreciate Teasdale's lyric given the fact that the "poems do not present the unexpected intuition, do not flash their light into depth of subconsciousness and make us thrill with a sense of discovery and secret fire."[26] Yet she too could criticize the poems for their lack of "intellectual passion" and psychological probing, although it was an aspect that Teasdale had deliberately eschewed in her work.

What is important to note is that such a demand for intellectual content had rarely before now appeared in poetry criticism. The models that Teasdale had emulated, as Aiken rightly pointed out, had focused primarily on purity of emotion, musicality, and memorable lines, and had, in fact, ruled out the complex, the clever, and the unusual. And in these areas Teasdale had achieved heights of expression. But perhaps more important was the fact that the element of thought was not entirely absent from her poetry. It was not, however, the kind of thinking that intruded itself on the reader; rather, as Teasdale had written, "The poet should try to give his poem the quiet swiftness of a flame"[27] with the full meaning "coming only on reflection." Unfortunately, many critics did not bother to reflect, or it did not occur to them to think about such apparently lucid, limpid quatrains.

Poets such as Teasdale faced a dilemma. All of her years of writing poetry had been directed to developing her skills according to standards shaped by the late Victorians. Modify them she could and did, but as she approached her fortieth birthday, her rebellious days were over, and it did not seem possible that she could revolutionize her style, even if she wanted to. And there is little reason to believe that she wanted to.

Her awareness of the changes in poetry must have deepened her autumnal mood and given her a sense that a new era was dawning of which she could not be a part. But if the critics were looking toward the kind of poetry that could be "viewed as specimens to be dissected in classrooms and learned journals,"[28] as one scholar has put it, Teasdale could find a measure of solace in the fact that there was a reading public unconcerned with changing fashions in criticism who would continue to read her for the purity, intensity, and music of her work.

Chapter Eight
The Music of Stillness

The period immediately following the publication of *Dark of the Moon*, which was a tremendous success, seems to have been noted by Teasdale more by her fears of interrupted privacy and need for "keeping a reputation" than as a moment to bask in public approval. Little now seemed to relieve her overwhelming depression, which had deepened during these last years, and many of the events that occurred at this time only increased it. The one event that countered this atmosphere was her meeting with Margaret Conklin. A young college student, Conklin had written to Teasdale requesting a picture for a high school teacher who had fostered her budding interest in poetry. After a lengthy correspondence they met. For Teasdale, the relationship satisfied many complex needs. She saw in Margaret the daughter she had never had, thus a chance to be a mother and to fulfill that part of her womanliness she had thwarted. The young woman was also the self that she had once been—sensitive, hardworking, and committed to an appreciation of the natural world. And, in addition, she was simply a reliable friend at a time when Teasdale's circle had contracted severely.

The relationship grew, though carefully monitored by Teasdale's caution concerning her new acquaintance, and in the summer of 1927 they traveled together to England, where Teasdale relived through Margaret's eyes her own excitement at visiting the literary sights in Devon, the Lake Country, and London. The friendship continued when Conklin moved to New York. As William Drake has put it, "In Margaret, she [Teasdale] saw a duplicate of her youthful self before the failure of her life had paralyzed her, and it suggested the possibility of starting over." She was buoyed up by "the ebullient energy of Margaret's more liberated way of life. . . ." In her young friend's life she saw the possibility that women's fate might not necessarily be one of inevitable suffering."[1] The friendship also inspired a group of poems to Conklin, some based on her experience in life, such as "Advice to a Girl" ("No one worth

possessing / Can be quite possessed"); some appreciative, such as
"To M":

> Till the last sleep, from the blind waking at birth,
>   Bearing the weight of the years between the two,
> I shall find no better thing upon the earth
>   Than the wilful, noble, faulty thing which is you.
>
> You have not failed me; but if you too should fail me,
>   Being human, bound on your own inviolate quest,
> No matter now what the years do to assail me
>   I shall go, in some sort, a victor, down to my rest.
>
> (*MH*, 127)

The friendship could only temporarily alleviate Teasdale's depression, not cure it. But it was the one bright event in these years of
gloom.

Teasdale's depression may have been due, in part, to the troubled
lives and deaths of her friends. Perhaps because she had so little
contact with people and had made no new friends since the early
years of her marriage, the unhappiness of old companions assumed
a greater significance. Amy Lowell had died of a stroke in 1925;
Teasdale's telephone companion, Marguerite Wilkinson, attempting
to cure herself of fear and depression, had taken to winter swims
in the ocean and had drowned off Coney Island in early 1928—not
quite suicide, but a "willed" death. The Untermeyers' troubled
marriage, their love affairs, reconciliations, divorce, and remarriage
were disturbing to Teasdale not only in and of themselves, but also
for their effect on their son, whom Teasdale had known since his
childhood. His suicide at the age of nineteen in 1927 left her
distraught. Only John Hall Wheelock remained an active and supportive friend and he and Conklin shared the burden of caring for
her.

Her own marriage also seemed to be on shaky ground. As if to
dispel her lassitude and to assert some control over her life, as she
had told herself in her poems, Teasdale took a drastic step. In May
1929 she left New York secretly for Reno, Nevada, in order to
establish the residency requirements necessary to obtain a divorce
from her husband, which she received three months later. The move
came as a shock to almost everyone, even Filsinger, who was, at
the time, en route from Southampton to Cape Town. Although

Teasdale had originally hoped not to inform her husband until the action was completed, her legal advisers insisted that he be told. His anguished telegrams and letters were of no avail. Teasdale enjoyed a brief moment of happiness according to Wheelock, who said that when she returned to New York, she exclaimed, "At last I am free!"[2]

While it is necessary to speculate about the reasons for the divorce at this time, it is also necessary to realize that the issue is a complex one about which, given Teasdale's extreme reticence, it is possible only to make a few reasoned guesses. It is doubtful, in the first place, that she was ever completely in love with her husband; she would not have wavered as she did in the summer of 1914 between Vachel Lindsay and Ernst if her heart had been committed. More likely, she married because she considered that convention demanded it and that some magical sense of fulfillment as a woman would be achieved through marriage and motherhood. Perhaps more important in destroying the marriage for her were her own conflicting needs. On the one hand, she required a great deal of independence in order to pursue her career, but on the other, she needed a tremendous amount of emotional support. The odd mixture of self-reliance and dependency must have been difficult to cope with. Filsinger was extremely proud of her achievements and respected the privacy necessary for her work. Her independence, then, was probably not a problem for him. He was even able, during the early years of their marriage, to provide some measure of the peace and security for which she yearned. With the passing years, however, he was less and less able to do so. Perhaps he had hoped, half-magically, that the knowledge of his love and concern might cure her of the massive bouts of depression and their innumerable physical manifestations, which strained his efforts to comfort her, and when such a cure did not occur, he may have been discouraged in his efforts to continue. The pressures of his own work and the constant need for an income large enough to cover their expensive household took their toll on his energies, leaving less and less to cope with her needs. His long working hours and his business trips certainly were a factor limiting the amount of time they had to be together. This point was the one stressed by Teasdale as a main cause in her complaint for the divorce. But Teasdale's numerous trips and rest cures without her husband, frequently just as he returned from a prolonged stay, suggest that neither of them was prepared to discuss the underlying problems in their marriage. As their times together were more and more filled with friction, even the respect and affection they felt for each other must have been obscured. It is perhaps significant to note that before Filsinger left for a nine-month trip away from his wife, Teasdale had fled to Connecticut to avoid the hectic atmosphere of his preparations and Filsinger was unable to find the few hours to travel to Connecticut to visit her. He did not have the time to say goodbye.

It was Vachel Lindsay's suicide that must have been the most difficult event for Teasdale to deal with. Although they saw each other only when his public readings brought him to New York, and most of their correspondence after his marriage was carried on through Teasdale and Lindsay's wife, the affection they felt for each other was deep and enduring. Lindsay's stability had returned after his marriage in 1925, but the pressure of financial difficulties after the birth of his second child brought on a renewal of his depression, worsened perhaps by the daily dosage of phenobarbital he took for his epilepsy. Harriet Monroe did what she could, both with her letters and with money, sending $100 one time from an unknown admirer, awarding him a $500 prize at another time. He had resumed the public recitations of his poetry, which he abhorred but which brought in money. By 1931 he was at a low level and began writing long desperate letters to Teasdale, as of old, seeking from her creative inspiration and support. They met in November 1931 for the last time. Their meetings and the value to each of them have been described by Wheelock:

And Vachel turned more and more toward Sara, whom he had always remained in love with. And he used to come to New York on visits occasionally when Sara was desolate herself after her divorce, and Vachel would come to the apartment and Sara used to talk to me about it, the wonderful comfort she had just from Vachel's sitting there with his arm around her or holding her hand. Two unhappy people comforting each other. And he feeling deeply romantic about her, and she regarding him as one of her oldest and dearest friends. She got a great deal of comfort from that. . . .[3]

Less than a month later Lindsay killed himself by drinking a bottle of Lysol. The effect on Teasdale was devastating; according to Wheelock, "it shook the foundation of things." He dates her own decision to end her life from that event.

The divorce brought only momentary relief. She took on new projects—a collection of poems for children and, at Wheelock's suggestion, a study of Christina Rossetti, which began as an introduction to a selection of poems to be published by Macmillan and which seemed to grow into a projected full-length biography.

The Answering Voice

In 1926 Teasdale had arranged for the transfer of her anthology of women's poetry to Macmillan, the company that now published all her work, and a reprinted edition was issued by them following the publication of *Dark of the Moon*. At the same time they asked Teasdale to revise and update the collection by including works produced in the decade since the first edition. Although Teasdale had little liking for the tedious details involved in producing an anthology—the selection, the letters to authors and publishers to secure permission to reprint, and the arranging of the poems within the book, she undertook the project, in part at least, because of the added income it would bring.

A check of her reading notebook indicates that she had already read the bulk of the new poetry by women, so that her statement in the preface, that "the poems in the second part of this book have been selected in a leisurely way during several years,"[4] is quite true. Nevertheless, in her usual meticulous way she had Margaret Conklin bring her books from the library to make sure nothing worthwhile was ignored. She was not always pleased by the new directions, as she confessed to Jessie Rittenhouse, commenting in particular on Edith Sitwell, whose style she called "sawdust and vinegar."[5] The limitation of the anthology to only love lyrics also caused problems, for many women poets were now engaged in writing about other topics; she could not find a suitable example by Marianne Moore, as she regretfully acknowledged in her foreword.

In that foreword she noted that "the decade since 1917 has produced more good poetry by women than any other in the history of our language." And the poetry itself was significantly unlike its predecessors: "The work of today differs so radically in feeling from the work of twenty-five years ago as to furnish the clue to the reason for the unusual amount of verse written. Women have been forced to write because they found nothing to hand that expressed their thoughts."[6] The passion of love had not changed, she felt, and a new attitude toward it had resulted from "the growing economic independence of women consequent on education, and to the universal tendency to rationalize all emotion." She used the change in women's dress as an analogy to prove her point, contrasting the modern dress—"so spare, so restrained as to ornament, so casual"—with that of former times—"the amplitude, the elaborateness, the formality."[7]

Chief among the differences she noted was the fact that "one finds little now of that ingratiating dependence upon the beloved, those vows of eternal and unwavering adoration . . . the pathetic despair."[8] Instead there is "the woman's fearlessness, her love of change, her almost cruelly analytical attitude." It was, she was careful to add, somewhat ironically, "perhaps at times overstated" leading to "the strident or flippant notes that occasionally mar the poems." But she excused such excesses as "unavoidable until through long possession they had become unself-conscious."[9]

Teasdale mentioned in the foreword that the past ten years had seen "the full flowering of two women poets of very high rank," and although she did not name them, she undoubtedly meant Edna St. Vincent Millay and Elinor Wylie, the only two for whom she included three separate poems. In doing so, she contradicted a statement at the end of her introduction in which she said that "those in the first part [the original group] who appear in the second, I have regretfully restricted to one poem each." Millay had, of course, appeared in the 1917 edition, and if the stricture had been seriously meant, she would have been limited to just one poem in this new selection.

Teasdale also mentioned in her foreword that there were "a dozen others not unworthy to be considered" top rank. Using the standard of the number of poems included for any particular author, she seems to have meant to include in that group Louise Bogan, H. D., Helen Hoyt (also included in the 1917 edition), Aline Kilmer, Charlotte Mew, Muriel Stuart, and Genevieve Taggard. Others who were included in the original version and also added to the new one were Zoë Akins, Grace Hazard Conkling, Amy Lowell, Lizette Woodworth Reese, Jessie Rittenhouse, Eunice Tietjens, Jean Starr Untermeyer, Margaret Widdemer, and Marguerite Wilkinson.

In discussing in the foreword the poets included in the earlier edition, Teasdale stressed the importance of Christina Rossetti, Elizabeth Barrett Browning, and Emily Dickinson. In doing so, she made explicit her admiration for these writers, which she had left unsaid in her 1917 introduction. It is a significant comment for, while the number of poems by Rossetti and Browning that were used might indicate her appreciation, the same is not true for Dickinson. The comment seems to indicate that her regard for Dickinson's poetry had grown during the ten years, encouraging readers to look for influences on her poetry.

A curious difference between this edition and the earlier one was the addition of two poems to part 1, so that the original group of one hundred poems was enlarged to one hundred and two. No mention of this change was made by Teasdale who apparently was attempting to rectify an earlier error of omission without calling attention to it. The newly added poems were "Remembrance" by Emily Brontë and "The Land O' the Leal" by Carolina, Lady Nairne.

Stars Tonight

A book of poems for children was the first major project undertaken after her divorce. Of the twenty-five poems she assembled for it, only three were actually newly written: "The Falling Star," "To Arcturus Returning," and "Night." Seven poems were reclaimed from among the unpublished ones in her notebook while the rest were extracted from previous volumes. The book was delicately illustrated by Dorothy Lathrop to match the verses with black-and-white pictures of small animals, birds, flowers and fairies, angelic figures, and dreamy children under starry skies. Although Teasdale attempted to provide a cheerful note by including some of her brighter poems, such as "On the Sussex Downs" and "Summer Evening," the mood is wintry, the colors subdued, the accent on memory and loss. It seems to be a repository for all her wistful melancholy with only the music of the lines to redeem the poems from sentimentality.

Two of the poems are "catalog" poems that children frequently enjoy. "Late October" lists five kinds of wildflowers in a scene of dying leaves, birds flying south, and a squirrel gathering nuts for the winter. The child-narrator tells the flowers to go before the snow comes, and when they do not heed her she realizes that "the others thought of to-morrow, but they / Only remembered yesterday," a sad sort of message. "Rhyme of November Stars" lists the stars by name attributing special qualities to each—one is lonely, some are timid, others are gold and queenly, or dusky dark and kingly. It is nothing more than a pretty survey of the heavens, without the final eight lines of the original version written in 1919 when she was studying astronomy in Santa Barbara, which question the plan of the universe:

> Your steadfast immortality
> Half angers and half comforts me,
> Serenely ordered, on and on
> You will shine—I shall be gone.
> (Poetry Notebook)

But the mood of that omitted epilogue informs many of the other poems. A typical example is "The Falling Star":

> I saw a star slide down the sky,
> Blinding the north as it went by,
> Too burning and too quick to hold,
> Too lovely to be bought or sold,
> Good only to make wishes on
> And then forever to be gone.
> (*MH*, 119)

Although the moment of brightness moving into dark is described rather than presented, the poem captures some of the sense of the elusive beauty of the scene.

Biography of Christina Rossetti

The major project that Teasdale undertook in these last years was a study of the poet who had most strongly influenced her own development and it soon occupied the bulk of her working hours. Teasdale's method of research reflected her careful workmanship. She kept a record of her reading and thoughts in a notebook, meticulously adding an index to her notes, giving page numbers for several key topics. [10] Headings included: C. R.'s illnesses, 88; Additional Notes on THE GERM, 81; Travels, 99. She listed books she "read or glanced at" on lefthand pages and quotations or notes on the right side. She covered a wide variety of material. Books about the Rossettis included *The Pre-Raphaelites* and *Rossetti* by Hueffer, *Recollections of D. G. R.* by Hall Caine; *Vers la Joie, Ames Paiennes,* and *Ames Chretiennes* by Lucie Felix-Faure Goyan; an essay in *Critical Kit Kats* by Edmund Gosse; Ford Madox Brown's *Diary;* and Ruskin's *Rossetti,* as well as family letters. She made lists of "best poems in Juvenilia," interspersed with quotations such as "no hurry in her hands, no hurry in her feet," or ideas, like "obsessions with idea of renunciation" or "A Royal Princess, a long poem like Mrs. Browning." She made comments about the quality of some sources with "both very poor" marked against two noted books and wrote notes to herself such as "look up description of her manner and appearance in later life." The orderliness, however, soon collapsed as entries of various sorts mingled among the pages. But when a particular quote was included in her text she wrote "USED" across the entry in the notebooks.

In the summer of 1931 and again in 1932 she traveled to London to do further research. In her notebooks she described places connected with Rossetti's life, the house in Euston Square, Brown's house in Fitzroy with her comments, some of which were copied directly onto the pages of the biography such as the description of the "large spreading trees in Torrington Sq." Other notes suggest directions that she might follow in developing her portrait. One by Paul Valery from his *Introduction to the Method of Leonardo da Vinci* is significant: "All criticism is dominated by the outworn theory that man is the cause of the work, as in the eyes of the law the criminal is the *cause* of the crime. Far rather are they both effects." If Teasdale were planning to follow up on this idea, it would have led her to attributing Rossetti's development to circumstance and chance.

Teasdale was able to complete sixty-four pages of a revised manuscript. But in that lengthy opening section she had only gotten to Christina's early years. It is charmingly done, being Teasdale's own thoughts and recollections on visiting the house where Christina had spent most of her life, re-creating the look of London at the time of her birth, and the change of attitudes from the last of the Georges to the Victorian era. Much time is spent on imagining the atmosphere in the home—the volatile father, the quiet, patient mother, the arrogance of Dante, and a general scene bursting creativity and exuberance. A full account is given of the early lives of the mother and father in one section, followed by a description of the birth, christening, and then the early years shown with children, pets, and studying father all crowded into the one heated room of the house. The children's lives during visits to the grandfather's house in the countryside occupy another section, and the last complete section deals with the life of the growing children in London. It was a slow beginning, a traditional one for biography, but clearly more than was necessary for an introduction to an edition of the poems.

The factors that Teasdale chose to highlight suggest that she was using the biography as a way of reviewing her own life. She focused on the transitional nature of the times in which Rossetti lived, mirroring the great leaps that had occurred during Teasdale's. She emphasized the spontaneity and buoyant imagination of the child caught between the spirited father and the passive mother, the creativity of the brother Dante and the excessive religiosity of the sister Maria, suggesting the polarities Teasdale had felt in her own home. The views on marriage that Teasdale attributed to Rossetti may provide an insight into her own views. In the notebook she insisted with little factual information for support that Rossetti's failure to marry Charles Caylay had more to do with "a disinclination to marriage in general" than to the religious differences between them. Describing her as "a born celibate in spite of her impassioned heart," she nevertheless went on to say "if a man of great force and charm had chanced to love Christina, she would have forgotten her innate shrinking from marriage and would have married him forthwith."[11] She concluded, however, with "Neither of the two men who wanted her in marriage would have made her happy." When she transferred these notes to the text, she omitted the reference to a possible successful suitor.[12]

The discussion of the poetry that Teasdale planned led her to pay particular attention to Rossetti's illnesses and her retreat from social occasions, seeing her as a person who got through "the ordeal of life" by withdrawing into herself and finding solace in her art. Her limited experience of life was not a detriment, for she "carved her life carefully as she would have carved a gem. . . . In the loneliness of her own arrogant heart she made a shifting and exquisite music."[13] Although Teasdale claimed "there is no need to make an analysis or appraisal of the poetry," she obviously planned to do just that. She described the best of Rossetti's poetry, saying that "it will last as long as our language." The feature of Rossetti's poetry that she chose to emphasize was its "shifting and exquisite music," "effortless singing," "music in clear colors, fresh yet exotic . . . which rang

with easy rapture."[14] And it is the music that distinguished Rossetti
from Elizabeth Barrett Browning as her notes show: Rossetti's "music is to E. B. B. what a song of Shubert is to a street melody."[15]
In tracing the development of her poetry she noted her progress.
By the time she was twelve,

Christina had learned that verse can be made to convey precisely what you
want to say. But it was not until six years later that she ceased to be a
mere versifier. Then the change that made her a poet came almost over-
night. She learned the exquisite truth that a poem can convey what you
never dreamed of saying.[16]

The revisions from the first to the second draft indicate Teasdale's
concern with stylistic matters, making the prose more compressed,
but frequently she modified a too harsh statement. The major changes
seem to reflect the differing attitudes towards religion between
Teasdale and her subject. In the first version Teasdale reveals a much
harsher attitude toward the sister Maria and even to Christina's own
religious nature. She had expressed her preference for Rossetti's
secular poetry in the preface added to the second draft. In addition,
in the first version Teasdale had commented on the narrowness of
Rossetti's religious tendency, saying "broadminded religionists do
not write great devotional poetry." The ironic tone was softened in
the second draft to the statement "but her own intensity lifted her
into the realm of the great religious mystics."[17]

The portion of the biography that Teasdale had completed was
charmingly written and showed an awareness of a myriad of influences that still needed to be weighed and evaluated. It was, however,
no more than a start, with too much attention spent on the figure
of the father and not yet a sense of how to balance her presentation.
A more serious problem was the lack of sureness in handling Rossetti's intense feeling for religion. As one critic has written, "to
accept Christina Rossetti without accepting her devotional inspiration would be something of a feat,"[18] yet it was precisely at that
point that Teasdale seems to have been blocked. She wrote Eunice
Tietjens that it was as "hard as granite,"[19] and the wavering treatment of it in the biography suggests that it would have been a
source of serious difficulty had she had the chance to finish her work.

Late Poems—*Strange Victory*

Teasdale did continue to write poems but few are recorded in her notebook, a mere thirty-six in more than six years. There was, in addition, a group of poems written about her divorce, but they were destroyed. If the quantity was limited, the quality was extraordinarily high. In these few lyrics she detailed with rare honesty the varied emotional responses that spring from the acceptance of the human condition and its inevitable ending in death. The oppositions that she dealt with were the eternity of the world of nature versus the mortality of humanity, the expectation one holds out for life and the disillusioning reality, the acceptance of death by the things of nature against the human protest, the memory of past relationships versus the barrenness of the present. While her attitude has often been called one of resignation, there is a core of courage that makes her poems more rightly considered lyrics of quiet affirmation of the spirit in the face of the realities of human life.

The inescapable fact of aging and death informs almost every poem. It seems to dominate every scene she looks at as the natural world either echoes or mocks her responses. The brooks in "Age" grow quiet without protest as they move through the seasons; the hills in "Even To-day" will remain even after men's creations are destroyed, and the beauty of the seabirds in the harbor in "To a Child Watching the Gulls," only leads her to ask the youth, "You who are young, O you who will outlive me, / Remember them for the indifferent dead."

"In a Darkening Garden" captures this sense even as it balances the needs of life with the threat of death:

> Gather together, against the coming of night
>   All that we played with here,
> Toys and fruit, the quill from the sea-bird's flight,
>   The small flute, hollow and clear,
> The apple that was not eaten, the grapes untasted—
>   Let them be put away.
> They served for us, I would not have them wasted,
>   They lasted out our day.

(MH, 120)

Every item in the catalog has a meaning; every word carries both a literal meaning and a higher significance; every image is peculiarly suited to the life of the woman who wrote it. In her ironic self-deprecating fashion Teasdale regards the sum of her work as toys. The pen she used is linked to birds and the sea, key aspects of nature that dominate her poetry; the flute suggests the ability to change the sounds of the wind into song. The apple reminiscent of Eve and the Judeo-Christian ethic implies the understanding from the Tree of Knowledge, while the grapes with their association with Dionysus evoke the pagan world of pleasure, neither of which she has enjoyed. In having them put away, in order that they not be wasted, Teasdale is suggesting that future generations will pursue her same path, that she and those like her are part of a continuum. And just as the poet asks that these things be "gathered together," so the poem itself gathers life together by tying "night" at the end of the first line to "day" at the conclusion of the last.

She longs for an attitude about dying that will permit her to "let go, without a cry or call." She imagines what it will be like—in "Truce" as the ending of a battle, a repose in "luminous air, on which the crescent glows"; or in "Last Prelude" as "a rush of sparks in flight" or "lost in the swirl of light." She visualizes her own remains in "Ashes"—"so little and so lost." She imagines the possibility of the spirit remaining in "All That Was Mortal": "To say / What the deep says to the deep; / But for an instant, for it too is fleeting," and she even imagines herself viewing her world after her own death in "She Went Before the Night Came Down." In the original version in the notebook entry of the poem, the "she" was "I." The brief poem that opened the book expresses her fondest hope for her ending, in which the balance of the opposing concepts—light and dark, life and death—are caught at a moment of poise:

> Moon, worn thin to the width of a quill,
>   In the dawn clouds flying,
> How good to go, light into light, and still
>   Giving light, dying.
>
>   (*MH*, 119)

A significant change in her point of view occurs with poems that deal with silence. In her earliest works Teasdale had struggled between her desire to be a poet and the propriety of such a calling. In her mature years she accepted her role as poet, regarding it as a gift, but also a debt that she owed for her life. The pain of creating her songs was to prove unbearable, and in some of the poems in *Dark of the Moon* she began to develop the idea that silence had some magical property. Hearing music as she did in the natural world was itself sufficient and did not require her translating it into poems. In these last poems silence assumed a stature all its own, a significance that not only denied the necessity of poetry, but even precluded it.

In the sonnet "Wisdom" she yearns for the strength to be silent in the face of death: "Oh to relinquish, with no more of sound / Than the bent bough's when the bright apples fall; / Oh to let go, without a cry or call." She diminishes the difference between song and silence as both equally able to express "the last, essential me": "It is my music, making for my need / A paean like the cymbals of the foam, / Or silence, level, spacious, without end." Sound is the attribute of youth in "Age." This final version of this poem, entitled "Sad Wisdom" in the notebook, assumes even greater poignancy when contrasted with the opening lines of the original version, which reads as follows:

> All brooks sing in the spring,
> But in the summer cease,
> So I who sang in my youth
> Have come to hold my peace
> (Poetry Notebook)

The complete final version is:

> Brooks sing in the spring
>   And in the summer cease;
> I who sang in my youth
>   Now hold my peace;
> Youth is a noisy stream
>   Chattering over the ground,
> But the sad wisdom of age
>   Wells up without sound.
> (*MH*, 117)

The changes to the final version seem minor, the change of a "but" to "and" and replacing "have come to" with "now," but they do more than tighten the phrasing. "But" suggests an exception; "and" implies the normal course of events. "Have come to" indicates some effort; "now" makes it more of a fateful happening. The choice of "wells up" to express the appearance of "sad wisdom" is a phrase more closely associated with tears; the revision removing all extraneous words creates a tenseness that mirrors the silence, which seems like a silent cry. The association of song with childhood is also present in "In a Darkening Garden," where "the small flute, hollow and clear" is among the toys gathered "against the coming of night."

A minor four-line poem written at the Museum of Natural History and not included, entitled "For the Hall of Fishes," picks up the theme of silence, praising the fish who "keep the secret of the farthest past, / children of water, silent and serene." Now the image of silence is aligned to serenity, to peacefulness, suggesting, perhaps, that speech would bring the opposite. The combination of silence with the eternity in which these fish are placed—"They move and have their being in the vast / Ocean that teemed before the land was green"—suggests also that the immortality that she felt she might gain from her writing might also be achieved by a silent melding with the grander forces of nature.

The music that was once her poetry is seen in "Secret Treasure" as a private gift that she enjoys for herself even though she writes nothing for other people to read. It is a quality she discerns in nature. She asks the ocean in "To the Sea" to "sing no more" so that she need not measure the changes that have occurred to her and those she loved with the "unchanging sea." The sea gulls in "Calm Morning at Sea" and in "To a Child Watching the Gulls (Queenstown Harbor)" are images of splendor and acceptance, while Vachel Lindsay is an eagle "free of the weight of living." The hills in "Lines," a severely shortened version of the original poem entitled "The Mountains (Intervale, N. H.)," are like music that in a striking figure, climbs to rest. In "Last Prelude" music becomes a way of visualizing the ending a life:

> If this shall be the last time
> The melody flies upward,
> With its rush of sparks in flight,
> Let me go up with it in fire and laughter . . .

Music, she says in "Let Never Music Sound," should not even belong to humans:

> Let never music sound
> Unless an angel make it;
> Let stillness reign around
> Until a seraph break it.

True beauty is found in its opposite:

> No song was ever noble
> As the unsullied wide
> Prairies of silence sleeping
> In peace on every side.
> (*MH*, 117)

The mystical quality of music finds its ultimate expression in the poem chosen to end the volume, "There Will Be Rest," where in "a reign of rest" she will hear "the music of stillness, holy and low." The magical quality that once belonged to melody is now found in its opposite and the ultimate balancing of opposites is caught in "the music of stillness."

The title poem, "Strange Victory," is one of the most confusing that Teasdale ever wrote. The complete poem is only eight lines long:

> To this, to this, after my hope was lost,
>   To this strange victory;
> To find you with the living, not the dead,
>   To find you glad of me;
> To find you wounded even less than I,
>   Moving as I across the stricken plain;
> After the battle to have found your voice
>   Lifted above the slain.
> (*MH*, 125)

Drake believes that the poem is addressed to Filsinger and indicates her relief in discovering during their first meeting after the divorce that he was able to manage his life despite the pain she may have caused him. Its echoes of the last stanza of Matthew Arnold's "Dover

Beach" tend to confirm that opinion. Arnold's poem, written to his
bride on their wedding night, pleads

> Ah love, let us be true
> To one another! for the world, which seems
> To lie before us like a land of dreams,
> So various, so beautiful, so new,
> Hath really neither joy, nor love, nor light,
> Nor certitude, nor peace, nor help for pain;
> And we are here as on a darkling plain
> Swept with confused alarms of struggle and flight,
> Where ignorant armies clash by night.

Teasdale had not been true to her husband, thus denying him the
only protection in life that Arnold's poem could present. Yet her
husband had not suffered; he had moved through the battle of life—
the "darkling plain" in Arnold's poem, the "stricken plain" in
Teasdale's—and had survived.

Death

During her second trip to London in 1932 Teasdale became seriously ill with bronchial pneumonia. Despite her doctor's orders,
she arranged passage on a ship to New York. Weak and ill, ensconced
in a furnished apartment instead of her own, which was being
redecorated, she became increasingly depressed, feared that she would
have a stroke and become paralyzed as had one of her brothers. Her
sister and Margaret Conklin took care of her, with Wheelock frequently consulted, but her despondency did not decrease. She wrote
Tietjens that the illness seemed to be "a becoming time to make
my final exit."[20] The illness did not kill her, but the panic remained
and a nurse was hired to stay with her. In December she began,
according to Drake, accumulating a supply of sleeping pills.[21] She
went through her notebook, marking poems for publication and
giving a title to the volume, *Strange Victory*. As a last desperate
effort, she went to Florida in late December to stay with Jessie
Rittenhouse, who was shocked by her "dangerous state mentally."[22]
Two weeks later she returned to New York, where she arranged to
give her sister power of attorney after a broken blood vessel in her
hand brought to the fore her fears of a stroke. Margaret Conklin
wrote, "The night before she died, I was with her all evening. . . .

Never by a word or a look did she show me what was in her mind, though I knew she was terribly depressed. Late in the evening she sent me home because she thought I looked tired."[23]

They had spent part of the time listening to Beethoven's Fifth Symphony together. According to Wheelock, after Conklin left Teasdale told the nurse that she felt quite well and that the nurse should get a good night's sleep. At some point during the early morning, Teasdale filled the bathtub with water, swallowed all the sleeping pills she had accumulated, and lay down in the tub. She was found by the nurse at nine o'clock in the morning when she went in to wake her. The water in the tub was still warm.

Chapter Nine
Conclusion

When *Strange Victory* was published in 1933, it was reviewed respectfully by critics who noted the austere beauty and the extraordinary lyricism. But they were also somewhat patronizing. Babette Deutsch felt that "they take no cognizance of the problems, be they technical or ideological, which trouble the younger generation of writers. If Miss Teasdale was conscious that the world was awry, that consciousness did not find its way into her songs."[1] And Louise Bogan, while admiring "the moving simplicity of these final poems," questioned whether "a contemporary audience for lyric poetry may be postulated."[2]

These reviewers did not realize, as Teasdale had claimed in her study of Christina Rossetti, that the writer of "lyric poetry is always contemporary. He works in the changeless feelings of men and not in their changing thoughts that shift restlessly from decade to decade."[3] The fact that Teasdale used her images in "the universal and almost never in the exactly defined sense" was precisely the approach that permitted her to see human problems in a deeper, more fundamental fashion than those particular issues that troubled the writers of the 1930s. As Harriet Monroe wrote, Teasdale had attained the "perfect lyricism" in "a number of songs too fine to be lost in the coming crowded years. Her name, her quietly powerful personality will live in them."[4]

One of the difficulties in assessing Teasdale's poetry is understanding her use of images. Her range was narrow and her application deceptively simple. In her earliest poetry she relied heavily on classical and medieval material culled from her wide reading and revealing, apparently, little or no understanding of real life. A closer inspection, however, reveals that she was using this material for a unique personal statement. Her Helen of Troy was not the usual pawn of men's desires, but a strong determined woman bent on revenge. Neither of her "fallen women"—Guenevere and Marion Alforcando—regrets her actions; they only wonder at the behavior of other humans.

172

The visits to New York not only broadened her experiences, but brought a new range of images that should align her with the most modern of poets. The tall buildings, which gave a godlike view, the streetlights that rivaled the stars, the parks that seemed like bits of encapsulated pastoral, even the subways found their place in her poetry. The bustle of people, the frank and open hedonism of the city, as well as the misery of many of its residents informed much of her work.

It is the world of nature, however, to which she most frequently referred in her poetry. And here, too, her use of images has created misunderstanding. She focused on three major features—givers of light, sources of life forces, and carriers of messages. But within any given poem, she concentrated on only one aspect of the image, thus giving a sense of simplicity to her work. The sun, moon, planets and stars were the most obvious sources of light, often equated with some supernatural force. This force might be beneficent as in the brief "Autumn Dusk," or it might be a pitiless reminder of human mortality as in "Arcturus in Autumn," or a promise of beauty in "Night," or reassurance that such a divine force exists as in "There Will Be Stars." If a reader focuses on only one of these poems, he or she will have the impression that Teasdale regarded that image in only one way. It is only by reading these poems as a cluster that the complexity of Teasdale's thought can be comprehended.

This complexity can most easily be understood from her use of water images, particularly the ocean. It might stand for the impulse to sexuality and hedonism as in "The India Wharf," or it might stand for sterility as in "The River." It might mean submission to death or to love as in "Sappho II." It is an image of fear in "At Sea" or of love in "Spray." Its changelessness might be a reminder of death in "To the Sea," but it gives a sense of immortality in "Beautiful Proud Sea." Again, only by reading a cluster of poems using sea imagery can the complexity of Teasdale's thought be discerned.

It was the carriers of messages in nature that explain in part Teasdale's poetic practice. Even when she was still writing the adolescent "A Maiden," in which roses and birds carry messages to a lover, she could conceive of the sea wind as carrying Sappho's songs across time and space in "Triolet, III." This notion is amplified as she viewed her role as a poet as that of translator of the messages of nature, producing a creative effect in "Primavera Mia" or "To an Aeolian Harp." Birds, insects, the wind, rivers, fountains, all have messages for those capable of hearing them, and for Teasdale, the element that made them comprehensible was melody, or song. Such songs were magical, expressing ideas in sounds that she as poet tried to translate into words, but which nevertheless had to retain the pure musicality of the original. One aspect that they shared was the simplicity of that melody, the sheer memorableness of the song.

It may have been to maintain this sense of herself as a translator of the messages of nature that led Teasdale to prefer the musicality and the simplicity of her style to the more modern approaches that were being developed during her career.

The great themes of love and death dominated Teasdale's poetry, but in her treatment of them she sought to capture the intensity of her emotional response. It was probably this intensity that she meant when she spoke of "beauty." Beauty for her was a matter of perception. In her earliest poetry, the physical attractiveness of the actress Eleonora Duse provided the intensity of her portrayal of these themes. Later she would believe that the elements should be reversed, that it was love that provided the impulse necessary to perceive beauty, that is, to experience an intense emotional effect. When love failed to provide her with her sense of completion in life, she sought another way to express the sense of intensity in her art. The mode that she used was the moment of poise between two extremes, such as the moment in "Beautiful Proud Sea" when the watchers "Burn, like stretched silver of a wave, / Not breaking but about to break." The best of her poetry and of her thought was achieved in poems where this moment is captured, but even in her less successful works, it is present in the ironic twist with which many of her poems end. The apparent simplicity of Teasdale's poetry masked an intensity just as the disarming naturalness of her technique masked extraordinary artfulness.

Scholars and critics were for many years too concerned with the new poetry to pay close attention to the kind of work that Teasdale wrote. But there was an audience who continued to buy Teasdale's books. The period of the greatest sales from her books not counting the posthumous volumes, was during 1931 and 1932.[5] And her *Collected Poems,* originally published in 1937, went through twenty-three printings between then and 1966, when it was reissued with an introduction by the poet and critic Marya Zaturenska, and that edition, too, continued to sell steadily. This popularity did not necessarily ingratiate Teasdale with the critics, who asserted a significant difference between "high culture" and "popular culture," assigning Teasdale's sales, as Louis Untermeyer put it, to "valentines and keepsakes."[6] But these critics failed to realize that many a lesser lyric poet whose work had once enjoyed momentary fame has faded from public view while a few names obviously struck a note with a discerning group of poetry lovers, suggesting that popularity did not necessarily mean mindless sentimentality. Among these, Teasdale's name stands with those of Millay and Wylie as poets whose works offer sources of enduring beauty.

In the past three decades critical attention has begun to reassess the nature of Teasdale's achievement. The biography by Margaret Carpenter in 1960 supplied a fuller understanding of Teasdale's life, particularly in her early years, and Zaturenska's introduction to the *Collected Poems* suggested avenues to a more critical appreciation of Teasdale's work. Rosemary Sprague in 1969 and Jean Gould in 1980 have provided appreciative studies. More significant have been William Drake's perceptive and thorough biography in 1979 and his new edition of the collected poems entitled *Mirror of the Heart,* which focuses more than the previous version on her later, mature poems and includes many from magazines and her notebook that were previously unavailable.

Feminist critics have been slower to recognize Teasdale's contribution. Emily Stipes Watts in her survey of poetry by American women has given scant attention to Teasdale's work[7] and Florence Howe and Ellen Bass have ignored her completely in their anthology.[8] Cheryl Walker, however, has given due consideration to Teasdale in her study *The Nightingale's Burden,*[9] although she sees her as a failure in the fight against women's powerless position. It should be remembered, however, as Carolyn Burke has said, that "it would not do to lament the female poet's self-effacement, her lack of self-assertion, or even her failure to speak in an identifiably female voice. Such approaches would be projections of our own concerns back onto writing of an earlier period."[10] And it is also necessary to recognize that in her early monologues, Teasdale proposed as models women who dared to use power and who chose to follow their own paths. Her later poems also show an awareness of the crippling effect of social conventions on women and more particularly the failure of the accepted role of the married woman to suit their needs and aspirations. If her statements are carefully veiled by a dignified reticence, they are nonetheless there and perhaps more poignant for their disguise.

Established critics have been equally slow to appreciate Teasdale's work. Hyatt Waggoner had only three pages for Teasdale in his monumental *American Poets from the Puritans to the Present*[11] and Roy Harvey Pearce none at all.[12] In part, their failure reflects the difficulty of analyzing lyric poetry, for many other equally fine lyricists also are given short shrift in their works. It is a cliché to say that lyric poetry defies analysis, but perhaps it is possible to indicate some aspects of its appeal. If, for instance, there were a fuller understanding of the deeper powers of melody on the human psyche, it might be possible to grant greater stature to the great music makers among poets. This was Teasdale's supreme gift, a gift that, as Zaturenska put it, "if it was not genius, certainly resembled it."[13] Recent history has shown us the power of song to move masses of people for patriotic or social causes, and the more refined use of it in lyric poetry needs to be more closely assessed. In the meantime, Sara Teasdale's lyrics will continue to appeal to all those who instinctively value the "magic of melody."

Notes and References

In citing specific poems, reference will be made whenever possible to *Mirror of the Heart: Poems of Sara Teasdale,* edited and introduced by William Drake (New York: Macmillan, 1984) and indicated in the text as *MH.* Poems not included in that edition will be cited from *Collected Poems of Sara Teasdale* (New York: Macmillan, 1966) and indicated in the text as *CP.* Poems not available in either of these sources will be cited from the volumes in which they originally appeared and the name of the particular volume will be given in the text. Complete publishing information appears in the bibliography.

Preface

    1. Ezra Pound, quoted by Hyatt Waggoner in *American Poets from the Puritans to the Present* (Boston: Houghton Mifflin, 1968), 333.

    2. Theodore Roethke, "The Poetry of Louise Bogan," quoted by Sandra Gilbert and Susan Gubar, *Shakespeare's Sisters: Feminist Essays on Women Poets* (Bloomington: Indiana University Press, 1979), xvii.

Chapter One

    1. This quotation and all subsequent quotations from the Rossetti notebook and the two drafts of "Christina Rossetti: An Intimate Portrait," are from manuscripts in the Library of Wellesley College and are printed with permission of the library.

    2. Charmenz S. Lenhart, *Musical Influences on American Poetry* (Athens: University of Georgia Press, 1956), 20.

    3. Rossetti manuscript, 2d draft, 62.

Chapter Two

    1. Margaret Haley Carpenter, *Sara Teasdale, A Biography* (New York: The Schulte Publishing Co., 1960), 110–11.

    2. Louis Untermeyer, *From Another World* (New York: Harcourt, Brace & Co., 1939), 158.

    3. Poetry Notebook. All quotations from the poetry notebook are courtesy of the Beinecke Library, Yale University.

    4. William Drake, *Sara Teasdale: Woman and Poet* (San Francisco: Harper and Row, 1979), 8.

    5. Drake, *Sara Teasdale,* opposite page 176.

6. Eunice Tietjens, *The World at My Shoulder* (New York: Macmillan, 1938), 26.

7. Reading Notebook. All quotations from the reading notebook are courtesy of the Beinecke Library, Yale University.

8. Carpenter, *Teasdale,* 29.

9. Letter to John Myers O'Hara, 25 April 1908. This and all subsequent quotations from the letters to John Myers O'Hara are courtesy of the Newberry Library, Chicago.

10. Travel Diary, 1905. All quotations from the travel diary are courtesy of the Beinecke Library, Yale University.

11. Carpenter, *Teasdale,* 29.

12. Anne Douglas Wood, "Those Fashionable Diseases," *Journal of Interdisciplinary History* 4 (Summer 1973):25–52.

13. Emily Showalter, *These Modern Women: Autobiographies of American Women in the 1920's* (Old Westbury: Feminist Press, 1979).

14. Cheryl Walker, *The Nightingale's Burden: Women Poets and American Culture before 1900.* (Bloomington: Indiana University Press, 1982).

15. Dorothy Dunbar Bromley, "Feminist—New Style," *Harper's* 155 (October 1927):552–60.

16. Carpenter, *Teasdale,* 71.

17. T. J. Jackson Lears, *No Place of Grace: Antimodernism and the Transformation of American Culture, 1880–1920* (New York: Pantheon Books, 1981), 142–81.

18. Ibid., 142.

19. Ibid., 77.

20. Ellen Moers, *Literary Women: The Great Writers* (Garden City: Doubleday, 1976), 143.

21. Walker, *Nightingale's Burden,* 118.

22. Lillian Faderman, *Surpassing the Love of Men: Romantic Friendship and Love Between Women from the Renaissance to the Present* (New York: William Morrow & Co., 1981), 159.

23. Carpenter, *Teasdale,* 33.

24. The complete sketch is reprinted in Drake, *Sara Teasdale,* 32.

25. Interview with John Hall Wheelock by William Drake, 15 February 1975. All quotations from this source are courtesy of William Drake.

26. Rossetti manuscript, 62.

27. Lenhart, *Musical Influences,* 20.

28. Hugh Kenner, "William Carlos Williams's Rhythm of Ideas," *New York Times Book Review,* 18 September 1983, 15.

29. Joanne Feit Diehl, "Come Slowly Eden: An Exploration of Women Poets and Their Muse," *Signs* 3 (Spring 1978):572–87. See also Lillian Faderman and Louise Bernikow, "Comments," *Signs* 4 (Fall 1978):188–95.

30. Adrienne Rich, quoted by Sandra M. Gilbert and Susan Gubar, *The Madwoman in the Attic* (New Haven: Yale University Press, 1979), 49.

31. Showalter, *These Modern Women*, 23.

32. Walker, *Nightingale's Burden*, 34.

33. Gilbert and Gubar, *Madwoman*, 51.

34. Quoted in Carpenter, *Teasdale*, 108.

35. Suzanne Juhasz, *Naked and Fiery Forms: Modern American Poetry by Women* (New York: Harper and Row, 1976), 5.

36. Drake, *Sara Teasdale*, 37.

37. Ibid., 35.

38. Quoted in Carpenter, *Teasdale*, 100.

39. Letter to John Myers O'Hara, 18 March 1908.

Chapter Three

1. Drake, *Sara Teasdale*, 40.

2. Lears, *No Place of Grace*, 47–58.

3. Ibid., 49.

4. George Miller Beard, *American Nervousness*, 1880; discussed in Lears, *No Place of Grace*, 50.

5. Lears, *No Place of Grace*, 50.

6. Ibid., 51–52.

7. Charlotte Perkins Gilman, *The Yellow Wallpaper* (Old Westbury: Feminist Press, 1973).

8. Drake, *Sara Teasdale*, 33.

9. Travel Diary.

10. Letter to John Myers O'Hara, 27 August 1908.

11. Ruth Perry and Maurice Sagoff, "Sara Teasdale's Friendships," *New Letters*, 46 (Fall 1979):103.

12. Letter to John Myers O'Hara, 24 March 1908.

13. Letter to Amy Lowell, 13 July 1916. All quotations from the correspondence of Sara Teasdale and Amy Lowell are courtesy of the Houghton Library, Harvard University.

14. Letter to Marion Cummings, 2 March 1909.

15. Orrick Johns, *Time of Our Lives* (New York: Stackpole Sons, 1937), 179–80.

16. Walker, *Nightingale's Burden*, 117.

17. The distinction is presented by Carol T. Christ, *Victorian and Modern Poetics* (Chicago: University of Chicago Press, 1984), 17.

18. Ibid., 18.

19. W. R. Linneman, *Richard Hovey* (Boston: Twayne, 1976), 81.

20. Discussed by Ellen Moers, *Literary Women*, 159.

21. Watts, *Poetry of American Women,* 76.

22. *Magazine Maker,* October 1911; quoted by Drake, *Sara Teasdale,* 83.

23. Ibid.

24. *Literary Digest,* 2 December 1911, 1055.

25. Walker, *Nightingale's Burden,* 21.

Chapter Four

1. *New York Sun,* 11 March 1911, p. 10.

2. Quoted by Carpenter, *Teasdale,* 159.

3. Alfred Kreymborg, *Our Singing Strength: A History of American Poetry* (New York: Coward McCann, 1929), 447.

4. The complete sketch is reprinted in Drake, *Sara Teasdale,* 75–79.

5. Ibid., 93.

6. Wheelock interview.

7. Jean Untermeyer, *Private Collection* (New York: 1965), 52–53.

8. Letter to Will Parrish, February 1914.

9. Louis Untermeyer, *From Another World,* 72.

10. Letter to Curtis Hidden Page, 23 February 1912. Courtesy of William Drake.

11. Wheelock memorandum attached to Teasdale manuscript, 5 March 1965.

12. Jessie B. Rittenhouse, *My House of Life* (Boston: Houghton Mifflin Co., 1934), 69.

13. Letter to Will Parrish, 21 July 1911.

14. Rittenhouse, *My House of Life,* 113.

15. Christ, *Poetics,* 27.

16. Letter to Jessie Rittenhouse, 5 January 1913.

17. Drake, *Sara Teasdale,* 97.

18. Quoted by Untermeyer, *From Another World,* 186.

Chapter Five

1. Louis Untermeyer, *From Another World,* 173.

2. Letter to Marion Cummings, quoted by Drake, *Sara Teasdale,* 99.

3. Quoted by Waggoner, *American Poets,* 336.

4. Ibid., 332.

5. Amy Lowell, quoted by Waggoner, *American Poets,* 338.

6. Ibid., 337.

7. Letter to Harriet Monroe, 20 March 1919.

8. *Boston Evening Transcript,* 5 August 1916.

9. Louis Untermeyer, *From Another World,* 171.

10. Ibid., 170.
11. Wheelock interview.
12. Untermeyer, *From Another World,* 178.
13. Anne Douglas Wood, "Those Fashionable Diseases," 38.
14. Letter from Filsinger to his parents, quoted by Drake, *Sara Teasdale,* 140.
15. *Literary Digest,* 27 November 1915, 1239.
16. Drake, *Sara Teasdale,* 98.
17. *New York Times,* 16 January 1916, 22.
18. *Nation,* 6 January 1916, 12.

Chapter Six

1. Kreymbourg, *Our Singing Strength,* 447.
2. Quoted by Carpenter, *Teasdale,* 227.
3. Wheelock interview.
4. Quoted by Seon Manley and Susan Belcher, *O Those Extraordinary Women* (Philadelphia: Chilton Book Co., 1972), 284.
5. Jean Gould, *American Women Poets* (New York: Dodd Mead and Co., 1980), 108.
6. Drake, *Sara Teasdale,* 172.
7. *Boston Evening Transcript,* 5 August 1916.
8. Letter to Filsinger, 14 July 1916.
9. Quoted by Drake, *Sara Teasdale,* 175.
10. Letter to Harriet Monroe, 20 March 1919.
11. Letter to Harriet Monroe, 24 October 1918.
12. Letter to Marguerite Wilkinson, January 1919.
13. Ibid.
14. Letter to Harriet Monroe, 29 May 1918.
15. Watts, *Poetry of American Women,* 14.
16. Preface to *The Answering Voice: One Hundred Love Lyrics by Women* (Boston: Houghton Mifflin, 1917), ix.
17. Walker, *Nightingale's Burden,* xii.
18. *Bookman,* October 1917.
19. Conrad Aiken, *Chicago News,* 10 October 1917.
20. Drake, *Sara Teasdale,* 168.
21. Gilbert and Gubar, *Madwoman,* 572.
22. Poetry Notebook.
23. Letter to Harriet Monroe, 6 April 1919.
24. Letters to Mr. Edwards, Librarian of William Jewell College, Missouri, 8 April 1920 and 23 July 1920. Courtesy of William Drake.
25. Letter from Amy Lowell to Sara Teasdale, 10 June 1919.
26. Letter to Eunice Tietjens, 1 April 1923.
27. Reprinted in *The Answering Voice,* 76.
28. Letter to Filsinger, 2 May 1920.

29. Drake, *Sara Teasdale*, 185.

30. The version quoted here is the one Teasdale published in *Flame and Shadow* and in the *Collected Poems*. A variant is published in Drake, *Mirror of the Heart*, 37.

31. Drake, *Sara Teasdale*, 204.

Chapter Seven

1. Drake, *Sara Teasdale*, 222.

2. Letter to Filsinger, 12 November 1920.

3. Letter to John Fletcher, 25 March 1921.

4. Quoted by Drake, *Sara Teasdale*, 175.

5. Letter to Amy Lowell, 17 August 1921.

6. Preface to *Rainbow Gold: Poems Old and New Selected for Girls and Boys* (New York: Macmillan and Co., 1922), x.

7. Quoted by Carpenter, *Teasdale*, 209.

8. Drake, *Sara Teasdale*, 212.

9. Ibid., 210.

10. Letter to Filsinger, 27 January 1924.

11. Quoted in Drake, *Sara Teasdale*, 214.

12. Notes sent to Professor Lewis, 13 March 1923, courtesy of William Drake.

13. Ibid.

14. Letter to Filsinger, 16 February 1926.

15. Wheelock interview.

16. Postcard to Amy Lowell, 25 September 1924.

17. Jean Untermeyer, *Private Collection*, 61.

18. Drake, *Sara Teasdale*, 222.

19. Letter to Amy Lowell, 22 November 1919.

20. Terrence Diggory, "Armored Women, Naked Men: Dickinson, Whitman and Their Successors" in Gilbert and Gubar, *Shakespeare's Sisters*, 135–50.

21. P. A. Hutchison, *New York Times*, 14 November 1926, 4.

22. L. G. Marshall, *Nation*, 1 December 1926, 608.

23. Marguerite Wilkinson, *International Book Review*, November 1926, 784.

24. Genevieve Taggard, *New York Herald Tribune*, 28 November 1926, 2.

25. Conrad Aiken, "It Is in Truth a Pretty Toy," *Dial*, February 1925, 108–14.

26. Harriet Monroe, "Comment—Sara Teasdale," *Poetry*, February 1925, 262–68.

27. Letter to Marguerite Wilkinson, January 1919.

28. Rosemary Sprague, *Imaginary Gardens: A Study of Five American Poets* (Philadelphia: Chilton Book Co., 1969), 101.

Chapter Eight

1. William Drake, "Sara Teasdale: Poet of Love, Reborn in Friendship," *New York Times Book Review,* 26 August 1984, 2.
2. Wheelock interview.
3. Ibid.
4. Preface to *The Answering Voice,* 2d ed. (New York: Macmillan Co., 1928), xi.
5. Letter to Jessie Rittenhouse, 27 March 1927.
6. Preface to *The Answering Voice,* 2d ed., x.
7. Ibid., x.
8. Ibid., xi.
9. Ibid., xii.
10. Rossetti notebook, 74–75.
11. Ibid.
12. Rossetti manuscript, 2d draft, 3.
13. Ibid., 4.
14. Ibid., 5.
15. Rossetti notebook, 45.
16. Rossetti manuscript, 2d draft, 62.
17. Rossetti manuscript, 1st draft, 1; Rossetti manuscript, 2–3.
18. Marya Zaturenska, *Collected Poems of Sara Teasdale* (New York: Macmillan and Co., 1966), xix.
19. Letter to Eunice Tietjens, 7 May 1928.
20. Letter to Eunice Tietjens, 5 October 1932.
21. Drake, *Sara Teasdale,* 290.
22. Letter from Jessie Rittenhouse to Julia Altrocchi, 14 February 1938; quoted by Drake, *Sara Teasdale,* 291.
23. Quoted by Carpenter, *Teasdale,* 320.

Chapter Nine

1. Babette Deutsch, *Books,* 22 October 1933, 8.
2. Louise Bogan, *New Republic,* 15 November 1933, 25.
3. Rossetti manuscript, 7.
4. Harriet Monroe, *Poetry,* November 1933, 96.
5. Carpenter, *Teasdale,* 327.
6. Untermeyer, *From Another World,* 164.
7. Watts, *Poetry of American Women,* 294.
8. Florence Howe and Ellen Bass, *No More Masks* (Garden City: Doubleday, 1973).
9. Walker, *Nightingale's Burden,* 142–47.

10. Carolyn Burke, " 'Supposed Persons': Modernist Poetry and the Female Subject," *Feminist Studies* 11 (Spring 1985):133.

11. Hyatt Waggoner, *American Poets,* 457–59.

12. Roy Harvey Pearce, *The Continuity of American Poetry* (Princeton: University of Princeton, 1961).

13. Zaturenska, *Collected Poems,* xxi.

Selected Bibliography

PRIMARY SOURCES

1. Unpublished Materials

Poetry Notebooks, 1911–1932. Beinecke Rare Book and Manuscript Library of Yale University.

Rossetti Notebook and two drafts of "Christina Rossetti: An Intimate Portrait." English Poetry Collection in the Special Collections of the Library of Wellesley College.

Travel Notebook, 1905, Beinecke Rare Book and Manuscript Library of Yale University.

2. Published Works

Sonnets to Duse and Other Poems. Boston: Poet Lore Co., 1907.

Helen of Troy and Other Poems. New York: G. P. Putnam's Sons, 1911.

Rivers to the Sea. New York: Macmillan Co., 1915.

Love Songs. New York: Macmillan Co., 1917.

The Answering Voice: One Hundred Love Lyrics by Women. Selected by Sara Teasdale. Boston: Houghton Mifflin Co., 1917. Revised, with fifty recent poems added. New York: Macmillan Co., 1928.

Flame and Shadow. New York: Macmillan Co., 1920.

Rainbow Gold; Poems Old and New Selected for Girls and Boys by Sara Teasdale. New York: Macmillan Co., 1922.

Dark of the Moon. New York: Macmillan Co., 1926.

Stars To-Night, Verses Old and New for Boys and Girls. New York: Macmillan Co., 1930.

Strange Victory. New York: Macmillan Co., 1933.

The Collected Poems of Sara Teasdale. New York: Macmillan Co., 1937. Reissued in new format, 1945; reissued with Introduction by Marya Zaturenska, 1966.

Mirror of the Heart: Poems of Sara Teasdale. Edited and introduced by William Drake. New York: Macmillan Co., 1984.

SECONDARY SOURCES

Bogan, Louise. *Achievement in American Poetry.* Chicago, 1951. Brief, insightful study of Teasdale's poetry.

Carpenter, Margaret Haley. *Sara Teasdale, A Biography.* New York: Schulte Publishing Co., 1960. Review of Teasdale's life, particularly fine in its coverage of her early years in St. Louis.

Drake, William. *Mirror of the Heart: Poems of Sara Teasdale.* Edited and introduced by William Drake. New York: Macmillan Co., 1984. Summary of biography with emphasis on her development as a poet.

——. "Sara Teasdale: Poet of Love Reborn in Friendship." *New York Times Book Review,* 26 August 1984, pp. 3, 28. Discussion of the relationship of Sara Teasdale and Margaret Conklin.

——. *Sara Teasdale: Woman and Poet.* San Francisco: Harper & Row, 1979. The definitive biography, thoroughly researched with important insights into Teasdale's life and work.

——. "Sara Teasdale's Quiet Rebellion against the Midwest." *Missouri Historical Society Bulletin,* July 1980, 221–27. A discussion of the negative influence of Midwest culture on Teasdale's work.

Gould, Jean. *American Women Poets.* New York: Dodd, Mead & Co., 1980. An appreciative review of Teasdale's life.

Johns, Orrick. *Time of Our Lives.* New York: Stackpole Sons, 1937. Reminiscences of Teasdale by a St. Louis friend and fellow poet.

Kreymborg, Alfred. *A History of American Poetry: Our Singing Strength.* New York: Coward McCann, 1929. Brief, contemporary review of her poetry.

Monroe, Harriet. *A Poet's Life.* New York: Macmillan Co., 1938. Recollections and evaluation of Teasdale's life and work by an influential friend.

Pearce, Roy Harvey. *The Continuity of American Poetry.* Princeton, N.J.: Princeton University Press, 1961. General survey of American poetry.

Rittenhouse, Jessie B. *My House of Life.* Boston: Houghton Mifflin Co., 1934. Autobiography includes discussion of their twenty-year friendship.

Ruggles, Eleanor. *The West-Going Heart.* New York: W. W. Norton & Co., 1959. Biography of Vachel Lindsay includes a discussion of their romantic and professional relationship.

Saul, George Brandon. "A Delicate Fabric of Bird Song: The Verse of Sara Teasdale." *Arizona Quarterly,* Spring 1957. Brief, appreciative study of Teasdale's poetry.

Sprague, Rosemary. *Imaginary Gardens: A Study of Five American Poets.* Philadelphia: Chilton Book Co., 1969. Perceptive comments on Teasdale's poetic achievement.

Tietjens, Eunice. *The World at my Shoulder.* New York: Macmillan Co., 1938. Autobiography covers years of friendship.

Waggoner, Hyatt. *American Poets from the Puritans to the Present.* Boston: Houghton, Mifflin Co., 1968. Brief, unsympathetic consideration of the poetry.

Walker, Cheryl. *The Nightingale's Burden: Women Poets and American Culture before 1900.* Bloomington: Indiana University Press, 1982. A study of nineteenth-century poetry by women that includes brief, but significant consideration of Teasdale's relationship to earlier writers.

Watts, Emily Stipes. *Poetry of American Women from 1632 to 1945.* Austin: University of Texas Press, 1977. Survey of poetry with short discussion of Teasdale's relationship to other women poets.

Wilkinson, Marguerite. *New Voices.* New York: Macmillan Co., 1924. Contemporary study of Teasdale's poetry by a critic and friend.

Untermeyer, Jean Starr. *Private Collection.* New York: 1965. Includes reminiscences by a close friend.

Untermeyer, Louis. *From Another World.* New York: Harcourt Brace, 1939. Assessment of Teasdale's life and career by an influential anthologist.

Index